God Wills Fellowship

OTHER TITLES FROM
LIVING CHURCH BOOKS

❀ ❀ ❀

Vol. 2: *When Churches in Communion Disagree,*
edited by Robert Heaney, Christopher Wells &
Pierre Whalon

God Wills Fellowship

Lambeth Conference 1920 and the Ecumenical Vocation of Anglicanism

EDITED BY CHRISTOPHER WELLS
& JEREMY WORTHEN

LIVING CHURCH BOOKS

Dallas

iv

Contents

Jeremy Worthen

PART I:
Historical Contexts

PART II:
Contemporary Theological Perspectives

PART III:

Reflections on Ministry and Practice

CONTRIBUTORS

✻ The Rt. Rev. Jenny Andison is rector of St. Paul's Bloor Street, Toronto.

✻ The Rt. Rev. Dr. John C. Bauerschmidt is Bishop of Tennessee.

✻ The Rt. Rev. Dr. Christopher Cocksworth is Bishop of Coventry.

✻ The Rev. Dr. James Hawkey is canon theologian and almoner of Westminster Abbey.

✻ Dr. Hannah Matis is associate professor of church history at Virginia Theological Seminary.

✻ The Rev. Dr. Charlotte Methuen is professor of ecclesiastical history at the University of Glasgow.

✻ The Rev. Dr. Ephraim Radner is professor of historical theology at Wycliffe College, University of Toronto.

✻ Dr. Michael Root is Ordinary Professor of Systematic Theology at the Catholic University of America.

✻ The Rt. Rev. Dr. Joseph Wandera is Bishop of the Diocese of Mumias.

✻ Dr. Christopher Wells is executive director of the Living Church Foundation, based in Dallas.

✻ Dr. Jane Williams is the McDonald Professor in Christian Theology at St. Mellitus College.

✻ The Rev. Canon Dr. Jeremy Worthen is team rector of Ashford Town Parish in the Diocese of Canterbury.

✻ The Rev. Dr. Jeremiah Guen Seok Yang is former president of Sungkonghoe University in Seoul.

INTRO

Introduction

Jeremy Worthen

ORIGINS

There is a photograph of the 1920 Lambeth Conference, perhaps taken from the gallery at one end of the Great Hall at Lambeth Palace. The bishops, their ranks of chairs set to face a desk covered with papers set centrally against the long wall, swivel their faces to look sternly at the camera, crossed legs on display in the front rows, formally though not identically attired in the ecclesiastical styles of the time.

The distance from what may be expected at the 2022 Lambeth Conference and beyond is immediately evident. Even with some significant absences, the gathering of Anglican bishops from around the world long since outgrew the historic space and decamped to the modernist campus of the University of Kent, on a hill overlooking the city of Canterbury and the cathedral that rises at its centre.

The almost uniformly white faces have been replaced by a welcome diversity of ethnicities that reflects the growth of Anglicanism over the past hundred years—away from its roots in Europe, where it has struggled with various kinds of decline in recent decades, as also in much of North America and the Antipodes. A greater informality and more varied kinds of participation will characterise what takes place in Canterbury as the bishops gather again.

Given this historical distance and the many welcome changes that separate the present from the past, why would it be at all important to reflect on Lambeth 1920 to prepare for Lambeth 2022? For the editors of this volume, the answer can be summed up in its title: "God wills fellowship," the first sentence of the Appeal to All Christian People issued by the bishops in 1920 following its approval as Resolution 9 of the Conference. Facing the ruinous destruction of the "war to end wars," political convulsions in Europe and around the world, accelerating technological change whose effects were beyond prediction, and revolutionary movements in contemporary culture: facing all of these, the bishops affirmed the gift of fellowship, through Christ, in God, with one another, and the responsibility that comes with receiving that gift to make fellowship "manifest," that is, tangible and visible, in social reality; at once interpersonal, ecclesial, and institutional. The texts of the 1920 Lambeth Conference taken together make it abundantly clear that we cannot choose between goods here. It is not possible to focus on making the divine gift of fellowship manifest in the Church and to neglect its presence in the world, or to rejoice in making it manifest within the Anglican Communion and have no concern for the relations between Anglican churches and other parts of the body of Christ. *God wills fellowship* for every dimension of our life, and the fellowship God wills must weave all together if it is to be truly manifest. We dare not betray the Church's calling to share the good news of peace with the whole world, but the lack of peace within the broken body of Christ is a fearful muzzling of the message with which we have been entrusted and demands our active and prayerful attention for the sake of the gospel.

Conversations across the Atlantic, gathering in a number of those represented among the contributors to this volume as well as the editors, led to the idea of a colloquium, to be held on the site of the 1920 Lambeth Conference. We would bring together scholars and students, bishops, clergy and lay leaders, to reflect on the significance of the Appeal (as we shall be calling it throughout this volume) in celebration of its hundredth anniversary and to generate creative dialogue and fresh insight. In early October 2019, around 40 people in total met for two days of study, discussion, worship, and prayer, with most sessions at Lambeth Palace and a public lecture at St. Margaret's Westminster, in the shadow of Westminster Abbey, where others also joined us. From different countries, different theological perspectives, and different churches, in our meeting together we tasted the truth of what we were considering: that God wills fellowship.

OVERVIEW

The papers given at the colloquium were not all of a kind, and the chapters in this book, which are based on them, vary in significant ways as well. Some are substantial academic studies; others briefer, more informal, and more personal responses. Some provide copious references, as both evidence for points made and invitations to further reading; others offer a sketch of insights and ideas without filling in the background in the same kind of way. All, however, take up the central challenge of the colloquium: the significance of the Appeal in the context of Lambeth 1920 for Lambeth 2022 and for the Anglican Communion, *and* for "all Christian people" and the wider world in which live a hundred years on.

The chapters are grouped into three parts. The first, "Historical Contexts," begins with **Charlotte Methuen**'s wide-angle situation of Lambeth Conference 1920 in relation to other developments of the time. The First World War and its profound effects on Christian spirituality, the experience of those engaged in Christian mission in Africa and Asia, and the emerging global ecumenical movement all deeply shaped the conference and the Appeal. Mooting questions that will recur throughout the essays in this volume, Methuen studies the way the Appeal revisits the Quadrilateral on the necessity of the episcopate for unity without denying the "spiritual reality" of ordained ministries in non-episcopal churches.

Next, **John Bauerschmidt** presents a theological study of the Appeal itself, setting out four of its guiding themes: penitence, fellowship, the diversity of gifts, and the re-working of the Chicago-Lambeth Quadrilateral. In every respect, the Appeal would help shape the period of extraordinary ecumenical fecundity to follow, not least by framing and motivating Anglican ecumenical thinking throughout the interwar period. Moving forward, the ecclesiological grammar of the Appeal became the normal way of speaking about the Anglican Communion.

Turning to post-1920 developments on the ground, **Jeremy**

Worthen picks up the story of how vision struggled to become reality with primary reference to the Church of South India. Here, in the classic instance of Anglican participation in a uniting church scheme in service of a putative ecumenical vocation, underlying tensions regarding the shape and necessity of episcopal office and the very identity of Anglicanism turned up problems that remain unresolved today.

In the final chapter in this part of the book, **Michael Root**'s retrospective evaluation of the Appeal in the light of the history of the ecumenical movement helps us further to identify successes and failures. In Root's view, a lack of realism about theological disagreements among its pioneers may have contributed to the sense of disappointment felt by many in recent decades.

Although the five authors of the chapters in Part I analyse historical developments relating to the Appeal, they all also comment to one degree or another on its significance for the Church of today. In Part II, "Contemporary Theological Perspectives," the emphasis is somewhat reversed, with the five chapters presenting accounts of Anglicanism's vocation here and now that creatively recover different aspects of the Appeal of 1920. **Ephraim Radner**, who gave the opening lecture for the colloquium, contrasts "thick" accounts of communion with "thin" ones. Finding Lambeth 1920 firmly on the side of the former, Radner gives a reading of the early chapters of Acts that roots historic Anglican's affirmation of a rich texture of ecclesial practices in the pouring out of the Spirit on the Church at Pentecost. **James Hawkey** also outlines a contemporary theology of communion, but in a somewhat different key. With Metz as a critical interlocutor, Hawkey suggests that because the Church is "a grace-filled koinonia, a participation in the life of the Holy Spirit," Anglicans (and others) may recover the Appeal's confidence in the historic episcopate as a gift for the whole Church. Here, Hawkey takes proposals for communion between the Church of England and the Methodist Church in Britain as a case study. **Christopher Wells** retrieves a broad ecumenical Augustinianism of the one Church as visible, invisible, and mixed to make sense of current Anglican discernments and to propose a path forward. Amid pressures to articulate truth and adjudicate inevitable inter-ecclesial contests, Anglicans at their best—from Richard Hooker through the 1920 Appeal to contemporary proposals—have marked incompleteness with an ear to the call of unity, so clearly inscribed in Scripture and the Catholic tradition.

The next two chapters in Part II shift the focus of the conversation somewhat away from the development of ecclesiology in church and academy. Both **Jeremiah Yang** and **Hannah Matis** call the reader to listen to the cries of those who are suffering in the world today and longing for justice to come. Yang articulates a renewed understanding of catholicity to overcome the deepening fragmentation within and between our societies, in the face of the destructively allied forces of "irresponsible relativism and the pursuit of strong hegemonic power." Matis calls for "Durable mutuality and compassion," manifested in practical initiatives of partnership between churches. Both authors are clear that the Church can only make the gift of its unity visible to the world as it stands in solidarity and fellowship with those who are suffering, not least in the face of the environmental crisis unfolding in our time at frightening speed.

In the final part of the book, "Reflections on Ministry and Practice," three participants in the colloquium consider what they heard there and relate it to their own continuing ministries: **Jenny**

Andison and **Christopher Cocksworth** as bishops of the Anglican Communion, and **Jane Williams** as a teacher of theology in the context of formation for ministry. Each is conscious of significant challenges in living out the vision of the Appeal today, yet also attentive to signs of hope. The call to mission, as an urgent and joyful task for the Church in union with Christ and in the power of the Spirit, animated the Appeal in 1920 and is again evident in these pieces., especially in Andison's piece, which highlights the importance of partnership and dialogue with the many vibrant churches in the world today that did not exist 100—or even 10—years ago. Cocksworth introduces the concept of *resonance* and proposes realistic steps that could be taken by Anglicans for the sake of the Church's unity—by welcoming the teaching ministry of the Bishop of Rome, and affirming whole-heartedly the "spiritual reality" of the ministries of those ordained in non-episcopal churches when those churches seek communion with Anglicans. Reflecting on the words from the opening of the Appeal that form the title for this book, Williams concludes Part III by urging readers to have confidence that "what God wills God will continue to give." Together, these reflections show how the truth that God wills fellowship continues to resonate in different parts of the Anglican Communion.

Unsurprisingly, there are overlaps between the three parts, and indeed fruitful interactions. The twelve chapters do not need to be read in the order in which they are presented, and readers may wish to head initially for whatever strikes them as of immediate interest and use. Nonetheless, the organisation of the material is intended to help the reader navigate a volume of rich variety the contents of which, we hope, have something to offer to people across the Anglican

Communion: those who are committed to teaching as an integral part
of their ministry, or to learning about their church's story as part of
their discipleship, as well as to students and scholars of Anglicanism
and the ecumenical movement.

ANGLICAN IDENTITY AND THE
TRAJECTORY OF ECUMENISM

As the chapters here vary in style, voice, and length, they also differ
from one another in the perspectives they bring to bear. Indeed, one
might ask to what extent these are differences in emphases only, rather
than revealing deeper tensions if not at times contradictions. Two subjects in particular might be identified as points of orientation against
which the contributions assembled here could usefully be mapped:
the identity of Anglicanism, and the trajectory of ecumenism.

The much-discussed question of the distinctiveness of
Anglicanism comes into view at various points in this volume. In Part
I, for instance, Methuen emphasizes the origins of the Appeal within
the wider context of the beginnings of the modern ecumenical movement. Anglicans may have brought something distinctive to this, but
only as participants in a development the energy, parameters, and direction of which were by no means exclusively of their making. How
significant, however, is the "distinctive" contribution of Anglicanism
to ecumenism? That is a question that spans all three parts of the book
and is bound up in turn with the second subject just mentioned, the
trajectory of ecumenism. If the Appeal can be taken to define or at
least summarise the distinctive Anglican way on the shared journey

towards Christian unity, is it a path that can be recognized as having reached its end a hundred years on, or a road along which it is vital that Anglicans continue to walk determinedly for the sake of the whole Church of God? As Methuen briefly indicates and Worthen shows more fully, differing views within the Anglican Communion about the value and viability of the Appeal as a worked-out vision and strategy for bringing unity to a divided church were evident from the outset. If confidence in its approach was broadly sustained by the Communion's leadership in the face of such questioning for the first five decades after it was released, it seems true that most Anglican bishops today do not naturally think and speak about the Church in classic Faith and Order terms. That said, the lexicon of the Appeal remarkably remains the lingua franca of Anglican ecclesiology when push comes to shove, as may be seen in the *Virginia* and *Windsor* reports, the Anglican Covenant, and numerous dialogues, as they take up successively the old questions of council and synod, federality versus communion, and structured apostolicity. We have not found another way to speak about these things.

Root places the proposed narrative of the Appeal in the context of a wider shift in ecumenism. Borrowing from Kuhn's analysis of paradigm shifts in the history of science, he argues we have moved from a "revolutionary" phase of ecumenism in the first seventy years or so of the twentieth century to a "normal" one, in which we need to grapple with long-term challenges that require realism and patience if they are to be addressed effectively. Wells's situation of contemporary Anglican debates within a wider ecclesial ambit stretching back to the earliest patristic synthesis about catholic structure and boundary somewhat similarly suggests that much about our questions may be old rather than new. In this case, we may more properly find grounds for encouragement than discouragement. For his part, Hawkey urges the theology of communion that emerged as a major influence on ecumenical thinking in the 1990s as still constituting the requisite theological framework for continuing ecumenical endeavour, whereas Radner sounds a more critical note in his retrieval of a "thick" concept of communion from earlier tradition, including the Appeal itself. Yang offers a powerful reminder that any consideration of the Church's unity today must embrace the differences between cultures and societies in a way that does not revert to assumptions about centre and periphery or rely on implicit claims about the power that some are entitled to exercise over others. The global nature of the crises we are facing, including the climate crisis, is for Matis, as for Yang, an opportunity to underscore the imperative of the church uniting in common action for the sake of the kingdom of God. One might ask, however, what is distinctively Anglican in these engagements with Christian unity, and whether it matters if there is nothing that can readily be described in such terms.

At least two accounts might be given of how Anglicanism over the course of the past hundred years has made a distinctive contribution to the search for Christian unity. One would be the characterization of Anglicanism as a "bridge" church, potentially spanning different kinds of divide but first and foremost joining Catholic and Protestant, or, in the language of the Appeal, episcopal and non-episcopal:

> On the one hand there are other ancient episcopal Communions in East and West, to whom ours is bound by many ties of common faith and tradition. On the other hand there are the great

non-episcopal Communions, standing for rich elements of truth, liberty and life which might otherwise have been obscured or neglected. With them we are closely linked by many affinities, racial, historical and spiritual. (Appeal, §II)

The bishops assembled in 1920 claimed equally powerful connections with both categories of churches, thereby placing the Anglican Communion in a unique and pivotal position for joining them together. It is a claim that has continued to be repeated by some Anglicans through the decades—in this volume, with qualifications, by Cocksworth; with scepticism by Root and Williams. Since Roman Catholicism entered the mainstream of the ecumenical movement in the 1960s, not long after the fuller involvement of Orthodoxy had been established, Protestant churches have found their own avenues to dialogue with the "other ancient episcopal Communions in East and West," without appearing to require any Anglican assistance, while it is not clear how far those other ancient episcopal Communions accept the Anglican claim to occupy a place alongside them. Nonetheless, a case could be made, hinted at by Andison, that there is something precious and remarkable in Anglicanism's capacity to encompass within its life those who maintain a deep spiritual empathy with Roman Catholic, Orthodox, Protestant, and Pentecostal, while still valuing the Anglican part of the body of Christ to which they belong; a part, moreover, that may be admired for its capacity—and/or valiant attempt—to hold together those whose affinities are so diverse, even apparently divergent.

The second account of Anglicanism's distinctive contribution to ecumenism—different, though not entirely unconnected—focuses on "faith and order" as a strand within the global ecumenical movement for which Anglicans have felt a particular responsibility and provided significant leadership. This becomes evident in Methuen's contribution and may be found in Wells's vindication of Augustinian conditionality in a latter-day Anglican accent. It was an American Episcopalian, Charles Brent, who worked tirelessly to call a world conference on faith and order, from the 1910 World Missionary Conference in Edinburgh, which he attended, to the first such event at Lausanne in 1927. The many parallels between the text of the Appeal and documentation produced by preparatory meetings in England for the envisaged international faith and order conference in 1916 and 1918 show the closeness of the relation here. Anglicans could not imagine a satisfactory form of Christian unity that did not encompass unity in faith and order, that is, in common doctrine and shared forms of church life; yet as they found representatives of other churches prepared to agree with them on this point, they were also drawn into a shared endeavour in which they learned and—sometimes—led.

Why should Anglicans have taken a leading role in the faith and order movement? One answer would be that, in Radner's terms, through the formation of the Anglican Communion they had learnt to value a "thick" account of ecclesial communion that included commitment to common doctrine and shared forms of church life. At the same time, it was a communion sustained without the coercion of legal authority, with generous space for a diversity of theological and spiritual emphases, significant variations in practice, and the bearing together of serious disagreements. That disposed Anglicans to believe that unity in faith and order was both necessary and possible for the Church in responding to God's call to make manifest to the world the gift of fellowship—communion—it had received in Christ.

Radner argues that the understanding of communion has become progressively "thinner" since the 1970s in the case of the Anglican Communion. It might seem that the price of accommodating disagreement has been a serious weakening of expectations about unity in faith and order, not least because conflicts about ecclesial authority mean that the question of how such unity can be established and expressed is itself profoundly contested. One might make a parallel case for the understanding of communion within ecumenical theology over the same period. Expectations of commitment to common doctrine and shared forms of church life have become gradually attenuated to the point where a hoped-for full communion between churches can appear to result in a unity that is not only hardly visible to the world but may barely register in the consciousness of most church members. As noted, Hawkey would take a more positive view of the potential, over time, for an opening towards communion, however apparently modest, to be transformative of our life together, in ways we cannot necessarily anticipate.

Both these accounts of Anglicanism's distinctive contribution to ecumenism—its role as a bridge and its advocacy of faith and order—connect Anglican identity with the history of striving for Christian unity. Not only do they have deep roots in Anglican history and polity: they picture Anglicanism as a stage on a journey, marked by a certain provisionality. It belongs to Anglican self-understanding to be a part of the whole, and a part that knows each part needs the whole. We may be less confident than Anglicans were in the mid-twentieth century that a new epoch could soon be dawning, in which the Anglican Communion would be radically transformed with the advent of a visibly united Church. But we might still claim that our Anglican vocation invites us to hold our identity lightly, as one that emerged from the contingencies of history in the providence of God. In that same providence, we might rejoice to find our identity taken up into a greater catholicity. Both accounts also intersect in the pivotal place they give to the historic episcopate: integral to the understanding of Anglicanism as bridge, it is bishops in historic succession who are pivotal both for teaching and handing on faith in the gospel and for maintaining the order that best expresses the good news that God wills fellowship for all humanity.

It is hard to read the faces—turned towards the camera lens at variously awkward angles—in the photograph of the 1920 Lambeth Conference. Perhaps it is not too hard, however, to find there some traces of inquiry and hope: inquiry as to what future generations might make of their endeavours, and hope that the things for which they had prayed and worked together might reach some kind of fulfilment. There is no doubt that a great deal has changed over the past century, and with it some things have been lost, perhaps never to return. But the idea that the Anglican Communion has a specific vocation to seek the unity of the Catholic Church and carries within itself a word for "all Christian people" that needs to be heard: that is not something that should be left in the subdued darkness of the past, however challenging it might be to let it face the searching light of the present.

PART I

Historical Contexts

✳ ✳ ✳

ONE

The 1920 Appeal in Historical and Ecumenical Context

Charlotte Methuen

The "Appeal to All Christian People," issued by the 1920 Lambeth Conference formed a landmark in Anglican ecclesiology, an important step on the road of the early ecumenical movement. Rooted in pan-Protestant responses to the First World War, the Lambeth Appeal was deeply shaped by the concerns of the mission field to overcome denominational differences.[1] Arising from Lambeth's

---

1   For the underlying tensions between the vision of unity expressed in the Appeal and that which informed the other ecumenical resolutions passed by the 1920 Lambeth Conference, see Charlotte Methuen,

"Sub-Committee for Relations with Non-Episcopal Churches," the Appeal sought a way forward on the question of episcopacy and the mutual recognition of ministries, points which were, and have remained, challenging in Anglican ecumenical dialogue. The Appeal provides an important insight into a period of rich and fruitful ecumenical engagement which would set the scene for the founding of the World Council of Churches in 1948 and for the ecumenical endeavours of all the major denominations in the post-second-world war period. It also offers an important reminder of what has been achieved ecumenically over the past century.

THE 1920 LAMBETH CONFERENCE: CONTEXT AND MODALITIES

The first Lambeth Conference took place in 1867, followed by conferences in 1878, 1888, 1897, and 1908. The pattern had settled to a ten-yearly conference, and the next was expected to take place in 1918. However, once it became clear that the war that had broken out in 1914 was not to be a short affair, the 1918 conference was postponed. When peace was signed in November 1918, the Archbishop of Canterbury and the preparatory committee agreed that it would not be possible to hold a Lambeth Conference in 1919: troops from around the Commonwealth were still being repatriated, and the

"Mission, Reunion and the Anglican Communion: The 'Appeal to All Christian People' and approaches to ecclesial unity at the 1920 Lambeth Conference," *Ecclesiology* 16 (2020), 175-205.

bishops needed to be in their dioceses to welcome them home. It was agreed that the conference would instead take place in 1920, lasting nearly five weeks, beginning on 5 July and ending on 7 August. Adding to this travel time by ship, attendance at the conference meant that some bishops were away from their dioceses for several months.

The conference assembled two hundred and fifty-two Anglican bishops from across the Communion, including the Communion's first Indian bishop, Vedanayagam Samuel Azariah (1874-1945), Bishop of Dornakal, and two African bishops, Isaac Oluwole (1852-1932), Bishop of West Equatorial Africa, and Adolphus Williamson Howells (1866-1938), Bishop of the Delta Pastorate Church and Assistant to the Bishop of Lagos.[2] *The Times* reported that the bishops came "from all parts of the world and of the most diverse traditions and experiences," and from very various circumstances:

> We need but little imagination to see them in their different dioceses. This Bishop is accustomed to travel over long stretches of land in the back blocs of Australia, another lives most of his time in the snows of North-West Canada, another must march through the jungle from one station to the next in Central Africa, another's work compels him to spend a large part of his time in boats which take him in turn to the widely scattered islands of Melanesia or the West Indies.[3]

2   The first African bishop had been Samuel Ajayi Crowther, bishop in Nigeria from 1864, who had died in 1891. The first Chinese bishop was Tsai-Sheng (T. S.) Shen. He chose not to attend believing that his English was not good enough. See Frank Theodore Woods, Frank Weston, and Martin Linton Smith in their *Lambeth and Reunion: An Interpretation of the Mind of the Lambeth Conference of 1920* (London: SPCK, 1921), 23-24.

3   *The Times*, 7 August 1920, 11, col. C.

The bishops gathered to address a range of themes, including:

※ Ecumenism, then known as the "Reunion of Christendom," which led to the Appeal

※ "Christianity and International Relations," with a focus on peace and the role of the League of Nations

※ "Missionary Problems," particularly "the establishment of self-governing, self-supporting, and self-extending churches" with representative structures

※ The development of Anglican provinces and an Anglican consultative body

※ "The Position of Women in the Councils and Ministrations of the Church," with an affirmation that the deaconess order "is for women the one and only order of the ministry which has the stamp of apostolic approval"

※ Concerns about "Spiritualism, Christian Science, Theosophy"
※ "Problems of Marriage and Sexual Morality"
※ "Social and Industrial Questions"

The bishops were deeply concerned about the social context of the Church. Church unity was imperative so that Christians could work together in combatting the challenges that faced society in the aftermath of the First World War.[4]

---

4 The bishops issued a series of resolutions and an Encyclical Letter, published in *Conference of Bishops of the Anglican Communion: Holden at Lambeth Palace, July 5 to August 7, 1920* (London: SPCK, 1920), which included a brief report from each of the committees. For the

The Chair of the Committee on Reunion was the Archbishop of York, Cosmo Gordon Lang. It was a daunting prospect, as Lang wrote to his old friend Wilfred Parker: not only did he have to deal with "the vast theme of Christian unity," but "I have a Committee of more than 60 Bishops to deal with, containing every variety of opinion, from Zanzibar and Nassau to Durham, and my heart fails when I think of the difficulties."[5] The committee divided into two sub-committees, one to consider relationships with "episcopal churches," that is, the Old Catholic, Roman Catholic, and Orthodox churches; the other to consider relationships with the "non-episcopal churches," including Baptist, Congregational, Lutheran, Methodist, and Reformed. The Appeal emerged from the sub-committee on non-episcopal churches. A draft was discussed by the whole committee. Finally, the Appeal was presented to the full conference, where it received an overwhelmingly positive reception.[6]

---

relationship of the Appeal to the Encyclical Letter, see the article by John Bauerschmidt in this volume.

5   Cosmo Gordon Lang, Archbishop of York, to Wilfred Parker, 9 July 1920, Lambeth Palace Library [hereafter LPL] MS 2883, fol. 245r-v.

6   For the recensions of the Appeal and George Bell's account of its drafting, see Charlotte Methuen, ed., "Lambeth 1920: The Appeal To All Christian People—An account by G. K. A. Bell and the redactions of the Appeal," in *From the Reformation to the Permissive Society: A Miscellany in Celebration of the 400th Anniversary of Lambeth Palace Library*, ed. Melanie Barber, Gabriel Sewell and Stephen Taylor (Woodbridge: Boydell, 2010), 521–564. Cf. Charlotte Methuen, "The Making of 'An Appeal to All Christian People' at the 1920 Lambeth Conference" in *The Lambeth Conference: History, Theology and Purpose*, ed. Paul Avis and Benjamin Guyer (London: Bloomsbury T&T Clark, 2018), 107-131.

Several key themes emerge from the Appeal. One is its deep sense that the search for unity was "an adventure of goodwill and still more of faith, for nothing less is required than a new discovery of the creative resources of God. To this adventure we are convinced that God is now calling all the members of his Church" (Appeal, §V). The Appeal was rooted in the conviction that each of the separated churches had its own riches and gifts: "we are all organized in different groups, each one keeping to itself gifts that rightly belong to the whole fellowship, and tending to live its own life apart from the rest" (Appeal, §II). Growing out of this recognition, the Appeal articulated a "vison," as the bishops explained,

> of a Church, genuinely Catholic, loyal to all truth, and gathering into its fellowship all "who profess and call themselves Christians," within whose visible unity all the treasures of faith and order, bequeathed as a heritage by the past to the present, shall be possessed in common, and made serviceable to the whole Body of Christ. Within this unity Christian Communions now separated from one another would retain much that has long been distinctive in their methods of worship and service. It is through a rich diversity of life and devotion that the unity of the whole fellowship will be fulfilled. (Appeal, §IV)

Related to this appreciation of the gifts held by all churches was the affirmation of "the "spiritual reality of the ministries of those Communions which do not possess the episcopate" (Appeal, §VII). This highlights another theme, ever contemporary in Anglican-ecumenical conversations: the role of the historic episcopate and the recognition, or not, of the orders of those not episcopally ordained. At the same time the Appeal expressed the Lambeth Conference's desire "that the office of a bishop should be everywhere exercised in a representative and constitutional manner" (Appeal, §VII). The role of the bishops in church governance was a topic for discussion. All these themes had emerged in ecumenical debate by 1920, when George Bell, as chaplain to the Archbishop of Canterbury, prepared a collection of *Documents Bearing on the Problem of Christian Unity and Fellowship, 1916-1920* intended to resource the bishops gathering for the 1920 Lambeth Conference.[7] The remainder of this article explores how these themes had been dealt with in those earlier ecumenical discussions.

THE FIRST WORLD WAR AND THE "ADVENTURE" OF CHRISTIAN UNITY

As already observed, the immediate social and political context of the Lambeth Conference, and therefore of the drafting of the Appeal, was the First World War. The experience of the war had been significant for the many clergymen who, as chaplains, found themselves ministering to troops drawn not only from all social backgrounds but also from all denominations, all faiths, and none. Some also worked, more

---

7   *Documents Bearing on the Problem of Christian Unity and Fellowship, 1916-1920*, ed. by G. K. A. Bell (London: SPCK, 1920) [hereafter *Documents (1916-1920)*].

or less closely, with chaplains from other denominations.[8] At the same time, the Great War had also caused many Christian leaders to feel a profound sense of failure. During 1914 and 1915, William Temple, then rector of St. James's, Piccadilly, from 1914 to 1917,[9] edited a series of *Papers for War Time*. A prefatory note preceded each of the first twelve works in the series and explained the basis of publication: "The present bitter struggle between nations which for centuries

---

8 See, for instance, Michael Snape, *God and the British Soldier: Religion and the British Army in the First and Second World Wars* (London: Routledge, 2005), 205-219; Edward Madigan, *Faith under Fire: Anglican Army Chaplains and the Great War* (Basingstoke: Palgrave Macmillan, 2011), 127-137, 197-201; Peter Howson, "Reflections on the Contributions of British Army Chaplains on the Western Front to the Discussion in the Winter of 1917-18 of the Nature of Post-war British Society," *Journal of the Society for Army Historical Research* 92 (2014): 60-72, at 61, 63-64; *idem*., "Visions from the Front: Discourse on the Post-war World among Anglican Army Chaplains in 1918" in *The Clergy in Khaki: New Perspectives on British Army Chaplaincy in the First World War*, ed. Michael Snape and Edward Madigan (London: Routledge, 2013), 169-182, at 179 (although he comments also that cooperation between chaplains of different denominations seems to have diminished during the war); J. H. Thompson, "The Nonconformist Chaplain in the First World War: The Importance of a New Phenomenon" in *The Clergy in Khaki*, ed. Snape and Madigan, 17-40, especially 35, 38. For the social and political engagement of chaplains in developing a post-war vision for society, see also Linda Parker, "'Shell-shocked Prophets': Anglican Army Chaplains and Post-war Reform in the Church of England" in *The Clergy in Khaki*, ed. Snape and Madigan, 183-198.

9 William Temple was subsequently appointed Canon of Westminster Abbey in 1919, became Bishop of Manchester in 1921, Archbishop of York in 1929, and Archbishop of Canterbury in 1942. He was the son of Frederick Temple, who served as Archbishop of Canterbury from 1896 to 1902.

have borne the Christian name indicates some deep-seated failure to understand the principles of Christ and to apply them to human affairs."[10] The authors and promoters of the series, the note affirmed, "are one in the conviction that in Christ and in His Gospel lies the hope of redemption and health for society and for national life."[11]

The papers published in 1915 included a revised prefatory note which asserted:

1. That Great Britain was in August [1914] morally bound to declare war and is no less bound to carry the war to a decisive issue;

2. That the war is nonetheless an outcome and a revelation of the un-Christian principles which have dominated the life of Western Christendom and of which the Church and the nations have need to repent;

3. That followers of Christ, as members of the Church, are linked to one another in a fellowship which transcends all divisions of nationality or race;

4. That the Christian duties of love and forgiveness are as binding in time of war as in time of peace,

5. That Christians are bound to recognise the insufficiency of mere compulsion for overcoming evil and to place supreme reliance upon spiritual forces and in particular upon the power and method of the Cross;

---

10 See, for instance, in the first booklet published in the series, William Temple, *Christianity and War* (London: Oxford University Press, 1914), 2.

11 *Ibid.*

6. That only in proportion as Christian principles dictate the terms of the settlement will a real and lasting peace be secured;

7. That it is the duty of the Church to make an altogether new effort to realize and apply to all the relations of life its own positive ideal of brotherhood and fellowship;

8. That with God all things are possible.[12]

A similar emphasis on the fellowship between all Christians and the need to "apply to all the relations of life" the Church's "positive ideal of brotherhood and fellowship" pervades the Appeal to all Christian People of the 1920 Lambeth Conference.

The *Papers for War Time* series articulated many themes that would shape the Lambeth Appeal. The most explicit reflection on war's impetus to unity was provided by the Scottish missionary theologian and advocate of unity, J. H. Oldham, who wrote of his hope that the war had given the Church "a new apprehension of the magnitude of the task to which it is called" so that it might "attain a larger, deeper unity."[13] Other pieces grappled with the implications for Christianity and the Church of what they perceived as the benefits of war as well as the evils it had brought. Oldham reflected: "Our people have experienced as seldom before in their history the beat and throb

---

12 See for instance the thirteenth work in the series, Percy Dearmer, *Patriotism* (London: Oxford University Press, 1915), 2.

13 J. H. Oldham, *The Decisive Hour: Is it Lost?* (London: Oxford University Press, 1914), 15. For Oldham, see Keith W. Clements, *Faith on the Frontier: A Life of J.H. Oldham* (Edinburgh/Geneva: T & T Clark/WCC Publications, 1999).

of a mighty common purpose."[14] His compatriot A. H. Gray, at that time a Free Church minister in an impoverished area of Glasgow, but about to join up for a short stint as a chaplain in winter 1915/16,[15] asked: "How can we do away with war, and yet retain the good effects of war upon the race? ... It is... an essential preliminary to any hopeful work for peace to recognise honestly the moral value that there is in war."[16] Gray asserted: "It is a sadder, poorer, and more confused world on which the sun shines to-day, but it is in many respects a better one. And it would seem that war has made it better."[17] Like Oldham, Gray believed that war "has the effect of knitting a whole nation in fresh bonds of fellowship and common purpose."[18]

The sense of purpose experienced through the war was also an important theme identified by the Oxford biblical scholar B. H. Streeter in 1915. In words that resonated with much preaching early in the war, Streeter affirmed: "Christianity is war. Every follower of Christ must serve on some crusade." Indeed, the Sermon on the Mount "is not to be read as a set of rules and regulations but as a battle-song—the

---

14 Oldham, *Decisive Hour*, 11

15 For A. Herbert Gray, see Sue Morgan, "'Iron Strength and Infinite Tenderness': Herbert Gray and the Making of Christian Masculinities at War and at Home, 1900–40" in *Men, Masculinities and Religious Change in Twentieth-Century Britain*, ed. Lucy Delap and Sue Morgan (Palgrave Macmillan, Basingstoke, 2013), esp. 170-172. Gray went on to publish *The Christian Adventure* (New York: Association Press, 1920).

16 A. H. Gray, *The Only Alternative to War* (London: Oxford University Press, 1915), 3.

17 *Ibid.*, 5.

18 *Ibid.*, 6.

Canticle of the Knighthood of the Cross."[19] Streeter saw Christianity as "neither a code of law nor a system of ethics; it is a summons to adventure."[20] Similarly, A. H. Gray saw faith as "a great adventure," which could drive out war:

> When nations come to understand the great Christian adventure, and learn that in pursuing it they will find their own highest life, then war will drop out of the world's life just as swords are dropped by men who want to paint, or make music, or write poetry. ... Then, indeed there will be peace in the smaller sense, but only because the world will be full of the noise and the joy of the warfare of God.[21]

---

19 B. H. Streeter, *War, This War, and the Sermon on the Mount* (London: Oxford University Press, 1915), 3-4. The language of crusade characterised much preaching in this period. See especially Albert Marrin, *The Last Crusade: The Church of England in the First World War* (Durham NC: Duke University Press, 1974), the title of which reflects this observation. Cf. A. J. Hoover, *God, Germany and Britain in the Great War* (New York: Praeger, 1989); for Scotland, finding similar patterns: Stewart J. Brown, "'A Solemn Purification by Fire': Responses to the Great War in the Scottish Presbyterian Churches, 1914-19," *Journal of Ecclesiastical History* 45 (1994): 82–104; Peter Matheson, "Scottish War Sermons," *Records of the Scottish Church History Society* 17 (1972): 203-213. Charlotte Methuen, "'The Very Nerve of Faith Is Touched': British Preaching during the Great War" in *La Prédication durant la Grande Guerre*, ed. Matthieu Arnold and Irene Dingel (Göttingen: Vandenhoeck & Ruprecht 2017), 63-73, identifies some different trends even early in the war.

20 Streeter, *War, This War*, 3

21   Gray, *Only Alternative*, 15.

War between nations would be supplanted by the cause of Christianity, properly understood. It was important to wage Christianity and peace rather than waging war.

As already observed, the Lambeth Appeal would apply this language to the task of unity, which it envisioned as "an adventure of goodwill and still more of faith, for nothing less is required than a new discovery of the creative resources of God. To this adventure we are convinced that God is now calling all the members of his Church" (Appeal, §V). The sense that the war had inspired a sense of purpose which now needed to inspire the Church both inspired the Appeal and formed a central theme in the text.

MISSION AND THE UNITY OF THE CHURCH

The significance of the 1910 Edinburgh World Missionary Conference for the formation of the ecumenical movement has often been observed.[22] Randall Davidson, Archbishop of Canterbury from 1903 to 1928, spoke at the opening session. Keith Clements observes that "he did not talk *about* Christian unity of cooperation, but embodied

---

22 See, for instance, Kenneth Scott Latourette, "Ecumenical Bearings of the Missionary Movement and the International Missionary Council" in *A History of the Ecumenical Movement (1517-1948)*, ed. Ruth Rouse and Stephen Charles Neill, 2nd edn. (London: SPCK, 1967), 353-402, esp. 363-363. Cf. much more recently Brian Stanley, *Christianity in the Twentieth Century: A World History* (Princeton: Princeton University Press, 2018), 12-35 and 127-133.

it in addressing his audience as 'brothers and sisters in Christ,'" with the effect that "scarcely imaginable possibilities might be burgeoning in the direction of more structured unity."[23] The 1910 Conference articulated the growing disquiet amongst missionaries, particularly evangelical missionaries, about the way that European divisions were being exported to the mission field. A "structured expression of international co-operation in mission" was needed,[24] laying the foundations for united, non-denominational churches in parts of Asia.[25] However, the presence of Anglo-Catholic delegates from the Society for the Propagation for the Gospel meant that the expression of these concerns was probably more muted than might otherwise have been the case.[26]

These concerns for unity in the mission field underlay the conference which took place at Kikuyu (now a suburb of Nairobi, Kenya) in East Africa in 1913, bringing together representatives of the Gospel Missionary Society, the German Lutheran Mission, the Friends Africa Mission, Seventh Day Adventists, the Church Missionary Society, the Church of Scotland Mission, the United Methodist Mission (UMM), and the African Inland Mission (AIM). The conference closed with a service of Holy Communion presided over by William

---

23 Clements, *Faith on the Frontier*, 90, 91.

24 Brian Stanley, "The World Missionary Conference, Edinburgh 1910: Sifting History from Myth," *The Expository Times* 121 (2010): 325-331, at 328.

25 Stanley, "World Missionary Conference," 329-330.

26 Stanley, "World Missionary Conference," 327, 329. Cf. Clements, *Faith on the Frontier*, 87-88.

Peel, the Anglican Bishop of Mombasa, assisted by J. E. Hamshere of the Church of Scotland Mission at which all were invited to receive the sacrament. Whilst Norman Maclean, minister of St. Cuthbert's Church, Edinburgh, applauded this service, regarding it as an "epoch-making event, ... the impulse of which will be felt throughout every mission field in the world,"[27] deep Anglo-Catholic misgivings were also vehemently articulated, led by Frank Weston, Anglican Bishop of Zanzibar, who protested that non-Anglicans had been allowed by Peel and Willis to receive the sacrament.[28] The 1913 Kikuyu Conference was followed by another in 1918, which proposed an Alliance of Missionary Societies in British East Africa. These 1918 proposals, together with a summary of the Bishop of Zanzibar's response to them, were included in Bell's *Documents Bearing on the Problem of Christian Unity and Fellowship,*[29] *which contributed resources for the Appeal. Taken together, these texts displayed different approaches to Christian unity amongst Anglican* bishops, an important point in the run-up to the 1920 Lambeth Conference.

The post war period also saw the development of proposals to

27 Cited in Julius Gathogo, "The Early Attempts at Ecumenical Co-operation in East Africa: The Case of the Kikuyu Conference of 1913," *Studia Historiae Ecclesiasticae* 36 (2010): 73-93 at 80, without attribution.

28 Frank Weston articulated his concerns in *The Case Against Kikuyu: A Study in Vital Principles (*London: Longmans, Green & Co., 1914). See Clements, *Faith on the Frontier*, 98; Mark D. Chapman, "The 1913 Kikuyu Conference, Anglo-Catholics and the Church of England" in *Costly Communion: Ecumenical Initiative and Sacramental Strife in the Anglican Communion*, ed. Mark D. Chapman and Jeremy Bonner (Leiden: Brill, 2019), 121-144, esp. 124-125, 126-130.

29 *Documents (1916-1920)*, text V and notes A and B, 37-47.

establish a united Church of South India, which included both Anglicans and the Syrian Mar Thoma Church. They focused on providing a single, geographically focused Christian church for the Indian subcontinent, rather than a plethora of missions relating to churches of different denominations. The United Church of South India had been established in 1908, bringing together the London Missionary Society (LMS) and the American Board of Commissioners for Foreign Missions (both Congregational), the Church of Scotland and the United Free Church of Scotland (both Presbyterian), and the Dutch Reformed Church in America. Later, the Basle Mission joined.[30] The South India proposals were offered as a response to "the challenge of the present hour in the period of reconstruction after the war, in the gathering together of the nations, and the present critical situation in India itself," which had highlighted the devastating effect of "past divisions."[31]

The Appeal acknowledged "this condition of broken fellowship to be contrary to God's will," whilst also recognising that "the causes of division lie deep in the past, and are by no means simple or wholly blameworthy." An appropriate response would include repentance, since "none can doubt that self-will, ambition, and lack of charity among Christians have been principal factors in the mingled process, and that these, together with blindness to the sin of disunion, are still mainly responsible for the breaches of Christendom" (Appeal, §III). That being so, Christian divisions needed urgently to be overcome, for the sake of the gospel: "The faith cannot be adequately apprehended

---

30 *Documents (1916-1920)*, 24 n. 2.

31 *Documents (1916-1920)*, 25.

and the battle of the Kingdom cannot be worthily fought while the body is divided, and is thus unable to grow up into the fullness of the life of Christ" (Appeal, §IV).

RECOGNISING THE GIFTS
OF ALL CHURCHES

The Continuation Committee established by the 1910 Missionary Conference provided the basis on which the International Missionary Council would be founded in 1921. It also provided the initial impulse for the World Conference on Faith and Order, an initiative of the Episcopalian Charles Brent, then Bishop of the Philippines (1902-1918) and later Bishop of Western New York (1918-1928). Brent was disturbed by "a disunited and competing Christendom woefully inadequate to the evangelical task," and by the attempts of Protestant missionary societies to convert the Roman Catholic population of his diocese, which he condemned as akin to sheep-stealing.[32] Initially unconvinced by the approach of the World Missionary Conference, and in particular by its exclusion of the Roman Catholic and Orthodox churches, Brent became convinced that the "Spirit of God was manifesting Himself with new power and so far as I could

---

32 Eugene C. Bianchi, "The Ecumenical Thought of Bishop Charles Henry Brent," *Church History* 33 (1964): 448-461, at 448. Cf. R. William Franklin, "Charles Henry Brent's Way of Unity: Faith and Order Origins" in *When Churches in Communion Disagree*, ed. Robert Heaney, Christopher Wells, and Pierre Whalon (Dallas: Living Church Books, 2022).

see He was preparing for a new era in the history of Christianity."[33] His response was to declare his intention of taking "immediate steps to bring into existence an organ" which would explore "deeper issues concerning faith and polity," which had largely been excluded from discussion at Edinburgh.[34]

National Committees were set up even before the outbreak of the First World War; the English Committee produced Interim Reports in 1916 and 1918 which were included in the preparatory documents for the Lambeth Conference. The 1918 Interim Report expressed the conviction that "visible unity in the Body of Christ is not adequately expressed in the co-operation of the Christian churches for moral influence and social services,"[35] a direct reference to the Life and Work Movement that had emerged during the First World War from the Movement for Christian Friendship under the leadership of Nathan Söderblom, Archbishop of Uppsala.[36] Such unity, they emphasised, "could only be fully realised through community of worship, faith and order, including common participation in the Lord's Supper. This would be quite compatible with a rich diversity in life and worship."[37] The proposed Faith and Order Conference worked on the

---

33 Charles H. Brent, *The Inspiration of Responsibility* (New York: Longmans, Green, and Co., 1915), 66, as cited by Bianchi, "Ecumenical Thought," 449.

34 Clements, *Faith on the Frontier*, 98; Bianchi, "Ecumenical Thought," 449.

35 *Documents (1916-1920)*, 11.

36 See Nils Karlström, "Movements for International Friendship and Life and Work 1910–1925" in Rouse and Neill, *History of the Ecumenical Movement*, 509-542, esp. 530-539.

37 *Documents (1916-1920)*, 11.

principle that "as we consider the needs and perplexities of others, we may gain a better understanding also of the means of our own convictions." Through this process of sharing, "it is possible to conceive of an ultimate reconciliation in which the convictions of all might find a place, and that such a reconciliation might provide a fuller view of Christianity ... than any one position standing by itself."[38]

Whilst a federal note was struck by the Bishop of Zanzibar's response to the Kikuyu proposals, which proposed that "non-episcopal bodies accepting episcopacy would remain in full exercise of their own constitution,"[39] the approach taken by the World Conference for Faith and Order was reflected in the proposals for a united church in South India, which sought to build the new church "not on any basis of compromise but on one of comprehension, where each body shall contribute its treasures and tradition to the enrichment of the whole."[40] The 1920 Appeal would reflect, without resolving, the breadth of these influences in its claim that "through a rich diversity of life and devotion... the unity of the whole fellowship will be fulfilled" (Appeal, §IV).

---

38 The World Conference for the consideration of questions touching Faith and Order, *The Object and Method of Conference* (n.p.: Commission of the Protestant Episcopal Church 1915), 29.

39 *Documents (1916-1920)*, 46.

40 *Documents (1916-1920)*, 28.

THE FOUNDATIONS OF FAITH

The Chicago-Lambeth Quadrilateral, agreed by the 1888 Lambeth Conference, defined the basis of "home reunion":

a. The Holy Scriptures of the Old and New Testaments, as "containing all things necessary to salvation," and as being the rule and ultimate standard of faith.

b. The Apostles' Creed, as the baptismal symbol; and the Nicene Creed, as the sufficient statement of the Christian faith.

c. The two sacraments ordained by Christ himself—Baptism and the Supper of the Lord—ministered with unfailing use of Christ's words of institution, and of the elements ordained by him.

d. The historic episcopate, locally adapted in the methods of its administration to the varying needs of the nations and peoples called of God into the unity of his Church.[41]

The first three articles of the Quadrilateral provided a statement of the foundation of theological agreement recognised to be fundamental in several of the approaches to unity collected by Bell in *Documents of Unity*.[42] The South India proposals reproduced them

---

41 Lambeth Conference 1888, Resolution 8, available online. For the background to the Quadrilateral, see Mark Chapman, "William Reed Huntington, American Catholicity, and the Chicago-Lambeth Quadrilateral" in *The Lambeth Conference*, ed. Avis and Guyer, 84-106.

42 See also Charlotte Methuen, "The Kikuyu proposals in their contemporary ecumenical perspective" in *Costly Communion*, ed. Chapman and Bonner, 145-162.

verbatim.[43] In contrast, the "Basis of Alliance" proposed in Kikuyu in 1918 was understood

> to consist in (a) the loyal acceptance of Scripture as our supreme rule of Faith and Practice; and of the Apostles' and Nicene Creeds as a general expression of fundamental Christian belief; and in the absolute authority of Holy Scripture as the Word of God; in the Deity of Jesus Christ; and in the atoning death of the Lord Jesus Christ as the ground of our forgiveness.
>
> (b) The regular administration of the two Sacraments, Baptism and the Lord's Supper, by the outward signs as commended by Christ.[44]

Here the first three articles were complemented by the more doctrinal statements regarding the authority of Scripture, Deity of Christ and the atonement. Similarly, although it did not include the sacraments, the First Interim Report of the English Faith and Order Committee integrated the first two articles into its articulation of the six "foundation truths" that it presented as "the basis of a spiritual and rational creed and life for all mankind". an Innate knowledge of God "to be found amongst all races of men," but reaching its "culmination and completeness" in Jesus Christ, the incarnate Son of God; the revelation of Christ as "the formative influence upon the mind and character of the individual believer;" the Word of God in the Old and New Testaments; the doctrine of the Trinity; the articulation of the

---

43   *Documents (1916-1920)*, 26.

44   *Documents (1916-1920)*, 39.

"historic revelation of God" in the Apostles' and Nicene Creeds; the affirmation that there is "no contradiction between the acceptance of the miracles recited in the Creeds and the acceptance of the principles of order in nature as assumed in scientific enquiry."[45]

The Appeal, for its part, affirmed as the theological basis of "the visible unity of the Church":

> The Holy Scriptures, as the record of God's revelation of himself to man, and as being the rule and ultimate standard of faith; and the Creed commonly called Nicene, as the sufficient statement of the Christian faith, and either it or the Apostles' Creed as the baptismal confession of belief; the divinely instituted sacraments of Baptism and the Holy Communion, as expressing for all the corporate life of the whole fellowship in and with Christ; a ministry acknowledged by every part of the Church as possessing not only the inward call of the Spirit, but also the commission of Christ and the authority of the whole body. (Appeal, §VI)

Its reiteration of the first three articles of the Chicago-Lambeth Quadrilateral with a rather more indirect appeal to the fourth recognised that the affirmation of the historic episcopate as a basis for unity posed a challenge to Anglican relationships with the so-called non-episcopal churches.

---

45 *Documents (1916-1920)*, 6-7.

NECESSITY OF EPISCOPACY

The Appeal's reference to "a ministry acknowledged by every part of the Church as possessing not only the inward call of the Spirit, but also the commission of Christ and the authority of the whole body," arising from the discussions of the Lambeth Conference's Committee for relations with non-episcopal churches, did not mention the episcopate at all. However, it was qualified in the Appeal by the question that followed: "May we not reasonably claim that the episcopate is the one means of providing such a ministry?" (Appeal, §VII). The episcopate, argued the gathered Anglican bishops, was "the best instrument for maintaining the unity and continuity of the Church." There was some discussion as to whether the episcopate was to be viewed as fundamental to the being of the church (*esse*) or essential to its well-being (*bene esse*), and the wording of the Appeal was viewed by some non-conformist commentators as being open to the possibility of the latter.[46]

The question of the episcopate emerges as central in many of the *Documents on Unity* collected by Bell in 1919. For the Bishop of Zanzibar, it was "not essential that we hold any one view of episcopacy on the doctrinal side, provided the fact of its existence, and continuance, be admitted."[47] The Second Interim report of the English Faith and Order committee argued that "the position of episcopacy in the greater part of Christendom as the recognised organ of the unity and continuity of the Church is such that the members of the Episcopal Churches ought not to be expected to abandon it in assenting to any

---

46   See "Lambeth 1920" (ed. Methuen), 528 n. 27.

47   *Documents (1916-1920)*, 46.

basis of reunion."[48] At the same time, the report recognised and affirmed that "there are a number of Christian Churches not accepting the Episcopal order which have been used by the Holy Spirit in His work of enlightening the world, converting sinners and protecting saints."[49] A similar attempt to balance a requirement of episcopacy with an acknowledgement of the "spiritual reality" and "spiritual blessings" of the ministries of non-episcopal churches would also characterise the Appeal (Appeal, §VII).

The form to be taken by the episcopacy was also a question raised in ecumenical debate. Responding to the Kikuyu proposals, the Bishop of Zanzibar affirmed that "episcopacy need not involve us in a monarchical, diocesan episcopate," and proposed that "the bishops should be freely elected, and should rule with the clergy and laity."[50] The first Mansfield Conference recognised "the place which a reformed episcopacy must hold in the ultimate Constitution of the Reunited Church" but believed that such a constitution would "also fully conserve the essential values of the other historical types of Church Polity, Presbyterian, Congregational and Methodist."[51] Similarly, the South India proposals preserved what were affirmed to be the "three scriptural elements" of ministry: the congregational focus on the ministry of every member, the presbyterian focus on synodical government, and the representative, executive nature of episcopal structures. The proposals were characterised by the conviction

---

48   *Documents (1916-1920)*, 12.

49   *Documents (1916-1920)*, 12.

50   *Documents (1916-1920)*, 46.

51   *Documents (1916-1920)*, 54-55.

that each form of church polity brought its own necessary gift: "all three elements, no one of which is absolute or sufficient without the others, should be included in the Church of the future, for we aim not at compromise for the sake of peace but at comprehension for the sake of truth."[52] The effect of these proposals would be, as Frank Weston had suggested, to include clergy and laity in the governance of the Church.

Similar concerns were articulated by the bishops at Lambeth who recorded in the Appeal that they "greatly desire[d]" that "the office of a bishop should be everywhere exercised in a representative and constitutional manner" (Appeal, §VII, VIII). This concern that the episcopate should be exercised in a representative and constitutional manner reflected the Protestant Episcopal Church of the United States of America, which had from its outset been constituted with a national General Convention which included lay representation.[53] It was also in line with changes to the governance of the Church of England. In 1916, the report of the Archbishops' Committee on Church and State was published, recommending the establishment of a reformed National Representative Church Council (which became known as the Church Assembly), including not only Houses of Bishops and Clergy, but also a "House of Laymen." There was to be a Parochial Church Council in every parish, with an electoral roll based on a baptismal qualification, deanery synods, and Diocesan Conferences,

---

52 *Documents (1916-1920)*, 25.

53 See S. D. McConnell, *History of the American Episcopal Church 1600-1915* (Milwaukee: Morehouse Publishing Co. / London: A. R. Mowbray & Co., 1934), pt. 2, ch. 3, available online.

also incorporating lay representation.[54] These proposals formed the basis of the Church of England Assembly (Powers) Act 1919 which provided the Church of England with a level of self-government by enabling Measures to be passed without recourse to Parliament, but it also for the first time ensured that lay people from congregations, and not just clergy, bishops, and Members of Parliament, were formally involved in the governance of the Church of England.[55] The Church Assembly met for the first time in June 1920. In August 1920, therefore, constitutional questions were very much in the bishops' minds.

RECOGNISING THE "SPIRITUAL REALITY" OF MINISTRY OF OTHER CHURCHES

As already observed, the Appeal's affirmation of the requirement of episcopacy as a basis for unity was complemented by an assurance:

---

54 See the Archbishops' Committee on Church and State, *Report*, with appendices (London: SPCK 1916). For its recommendations, see Dan D. Cruickshank, *The Theology and Ecclesiology of the Prayer Book Crisis, 1906–1928* (Cham: Palgrave MacMillan, 2019), 42-43; *Synodical Government in the Church of England: A Review*, being the report of the review group appointed by the Standing Committee of the General Synod (London: Church House Publishing, 1997), 125.

55 See for an account of the process Cruickshank, *Prayer Book Crisis*, 40-51. Compare also *Synodical Government*, 125-127, which points out that laity continued to be excluded from the process of making Canons; the Convocations of Canterbury and York retained exclusive responsibility in this regard. Although in 1920 they were granted powers to reform their constitutions, they remained exclusively clerical bodies.

It is not that we call in question for a moment the spiritual reality of the ministries of those Communions which do not possess the episcopate. On the contrary we thankfully acknowledge that these ministries have been manifestly blessed and owned by the Holy Spirit as effective means of grace. (Appeal, §VII)

This resonated not only with the Second Interim report of the English Faith and Order committee considered above, but also with a Memorandum issued in July 1919 by 137 Church of England clergy. Whilst reiterating that "episcopacy is demanded both by history and by the needs of Ultimate Unity, and is the only practical basis of Reunion and Reconstruction," the memorandum recognised "that those organised Christian Communions which accept the first three Articles of the Lambeth Statement [i.e., the Quadrilateral], but which are in our view deficient in Order through not having retained the Historic Episcopate, are nevertheless true parts of the one Church of Jesus Christ," and that "their Ministry, in and for their own Communions, is a true Ministry of the Word and Sacraments; and we acknowledge with reverence and gratitude the operation of the Holy Spirit among them, and in their Ministry." It concluded that "the Ministry and Sacraments of Non-Episcopal Churches are not inoperative as means of grace, but irregular from the point of view of historic Catholic order."[56]

The question therefore arose of how this perceived irregularity could be mitigated. Any way forward, as the Second Interim report of the English Faith and Order committee affirmed, should include "acceptance of the fact of episcopacy and not any theory as to its character." Moreover, this acceptance "should not involve any Christian community in the necessity of disowning its past."[57] In this spirit, Arthur Winnington-Ingram, Bishop of London, preaching in 1919 on proposals for reunion between the Church of England and the Wesleyan Methodist Church, proposed a form of ordination for Methodists involving presbyters and bishops. This was to be accompanied by a "form of protestation," which he said had been approved "by some High Churchmen as well as by leading Wesleyans," namely:

> Be it known ... that the ordination of AB ... is not intended by either party to express adverse judgement on the spiritual value of the ministry previously exercised by him, but to provide for the future that his ministrations shall have all the authority committed by God to men for that office which both parties may recognise without scruple.[58]

The proposed Concordat between the Congregational and Episcopal churches in the USA also took this approach, making it possible for Congregational ministers to received episcopal ordination and therefore to minister in both churches.[59]

Whilst the same principles underlay the proposals around

---

57 *Documents (1916-1920)*, 13.

58 *Documents (1916-1920)*, 51-52.

59 For the Concordat and its impact, see Peter G. Gowing, "Newman Smyth and the Congregational-Episcopal Concordat," *Church History* 33 (1964): 175-191.

ordination made in the Appeal, the approach there focused on the need for mutuality, and the first emphasis was on the willingness of Anglican clergy and bishops to receive whatever form of commission was deemed necessary:

> we are persuaded that, terms of union having been otherwise satisfactorily adjusted, bishops and clergy of our Communion would willingly accept from these authorities a form of commission or recognition which would commend our ministry to their congregations, as having its place in the one family life.[60]

With reference to recognising the spiritual reality of ministry, whether one's own or that of others, the bishops emphasised:

> In so acting no one of us could possibly be taken to repudiate his past ministry. God forbid that any man should repudiate a past experience rich in spiritual blessings for himself and others. Nor would any of us be dishonouring the Holy Spirit of God, whose call led us all to our several ministries, and whose power enabled us to perform them.[61]

This approach resonated with the response of the Bishop of Zanzibar to the Kikuyu proposals, in which he too had emphasised the mutuality of such ordination:

---

60 "Appeal to All Christian People," VIII.

61 "Appeal to All Christian People," VIII.

> If the non-episcopal bodies would ... consent to some Episcopal
> Consecration and ordination so as to enable them to minister,
> by invitation, in episcopal churches, he or his part would gladly
> come before any of their congregations, and accept any form of
> popular recognition.[62]

In the Appeal the Bishops affirmed a similar intention: "We shall be publicly and formally seeking additional recognition of a new call to wider service in a reunited Church, and imploring for ourselves God's grace and strength to fulfil the same" (Appeal, §VIII). In this way, the Appeal sought a more mutual approach, recognising the need for members of different churches to affirm and commission one another.

PRACTICAL COOPERATION BETWEEN CHURCHES

Appended to the Appeal was Resolution 12, which laid out proposals according to which Anglicans could engage with other churches. The bishops here sought to balance different views within the Anglican Communion. Bell's *Documents on Unity* included resolutions from several English conferences that took very different approaches, ranging from the repudiation of any form of joint service with

---

62 *Documents (1916-1920)*, 47.

"non-episcopal bodies"[63] through provision for special ecumenical services,[64] calls for pulpit exchange, and "reciprocal intercommunion" between the Church of England and Free Churches.[65]

This range of options would feed into the practical proposals associated with the Appeal, which authorised occasional pulpit exchange with ministers who were working towards unity[66] and opened

---

63   See the petition presented by the delegates of two conferences at Pusey House to the Convocation of Canterbury (1919), *Documents (1916-1920)*, 60, including the following points: "5. We ought not to take part in united services either in our places of worship or in those of the non-episcopal bodies. 6. It is not possible for us in any circumstances to preach or minister in the places of worship belonging to non-episcopal bodies, at any of their services .... 7. There are no circumstances in which we can invite members of non-episcopal bodies to minister or preach in our churches."

64   See "Co-operation with Nonconformists," being proposals of a Joint Committee of the Convocation of Canterbury (1919) in *Documents (1916-1920)*, 63-64: "clergy of the Church of England may accept invitations to take part in services other than those of the Church, provided—(a) that such services are of a special character and not part of the *ordinary* worship of other communions; (b) that the approval of the Bishop has been *first* obtained; (c) that in parishes other than their own, the incumbent has first given his consent."

65   See Resolutions of the Fourth Cheltenham Conference (1919) in *Documents (1916-1920)*, 66: "as a witness to the fact of Spiritual Unity, interchange of pulpits with the accredited ministers, and reciprocal inter-communion with the members of the Evangelical Free Churches, are desirable."

66   Lambeth 1920, Resolution 12.A.i: "A bishop is justified in giving occasional authorisation to ministers, not episcopally ordained, who in his judgement are working towards an ideal of union such as is described

the door to eucharistic hospitality,[67] but which did not approve "general schemes of intercommunion or exchange of pulpits,"[68] or celebrations of the Eucharist in Anglican churches by ministers not episcopally ordained, or Anglicans receiving communion in other churches.[69] The Appeal thus took an approach that lay roughly in the middle of the spectrum of proposals from the Church of England. It would form the basis of the work of ecumenically-minded Anglicans such as George Bell in the following decade.[70]

in our Appeal, to preach in churches within his diocese, and to clergy of the diocese to preach in the churches of such ministers."

67 Lambeth 1920, Resolution 12.A.ii: "The bishops of the Anglican Communion will not question the action of any bishop who, in the few years between the initiation and the completion of a definite scheme of union, shall countenance the irregularity of admitting to Communion the baptized but unconfirmed communicants of the non-episcopal congregations concerned in the scheme."

68 Lambeth 1920, Resolution 12.B.i.

69 Lambeth 1920, Resolution 12.B.ii: "In accordance with the principle of Church order set forth in the Preface to the Ordinal attached to the Book of Common Prayer, it cannot approve the celebration in Anglican churches of the Holy Communion for members of the Anglican Church by ministers who have not been episcopally ordained; and that it should be regarded as the general rule of the Church that Anglican communicants should receive Holy Communion only at the hands of ministers of their own Church, or of Churches in communion therewith."

70 See Charlotte Methuen, "'Fulfilling Christ's own Wish that we Should be One': The Early Ecumenical Work of George Bell as Chaplain to the Archbishop of Canterbury and Dean of Canterbury (1914–1929)," *Kirchliche Zeitgeschichte* 21 (2008): 222-245; reprinted in *The Church*

RESPONSES TO THE APPEAL

"Carried 3.15 p.m. Friday 30 July 1920 with 4 dissentions," reads a note on one copy of the proof of the text. "The Conference sang the doxology on the suggestion of the Bishop of Worcester."[71]

Lang reported to his friend Wilfred Parker on his relief at the completion of the work:

> Having got things through Committee, I was afraid that the remaining 200 Bishops, who had not worked together as we had for a fortnight of ceaseless toil, would cut the thing to bits. Instead of that, when I presented the Report it seemed to be taken out of my hands and what Neville called "a rushing mighty wind" seemed to sweep away difficulties and criticism, and instead of days of anxious discussion the appeal and its accompanying resolutions were adopted in less than one day with only a handful of Bishops objecting. I think most of us who were present will not forget that day, for it was difficult—to me impossible—to think that this wind was other than the wind of the Spirit: anyhow, I must believe that somehow God has a purpose in a thing which came with so much unanimity from 200 Bishops who really prayed and asked for guidance at a critical time.[72]

and Humanity: The Life and Work of George Bell, 1883–1958, ed. Andrew Chandler (Aldershot: Ashgate, 2012), 25-46.

71   LPL Douglas Papers vol. 1, fol. 410v.

72   Lang to Wilfred Parker, 10 August 1920, LPL MS 2883, fol. 248–249.

There was a palpable sense of achievement amongst the Lambeth bishops. In his closing sermon Thomas Gailor, Bishop of Tennessee and Acting Presiding Bishop of the Protestant Episcopal Church of the USA, affirmed the "wonderful unanimity with which 250 bishops from many lands reached agreement on the essential principles of Catholic reunion."[73] Positive reactions were received from John Wardle Stafford, a Wesleyan Methodist, who believed that it had "already stirred Christendom to the uttermost parts of the earth," and from Dugald MacFadyen, Secretary of the British Council for the Interchange of Preachers and Speakers between Britain and America, who viewed the Appeal as having shifted the emphasis of the fourth article of the Lambeth Quadrilateral "from the episcopate to ministry."[74]

The Appeal fed directly into the preparations for the World Council for Faith and Order, the preliminary meeting of which followed the Lambeth Conference almost immediately, running from 12 to 20 August in Geneva. Brent was present, along with fourteen other bishops who had travelled from the Lambeth Conference, three of whom (Boutflower of South Tokyo, Palmer of Bombay, and White of Willochra) had been involved in the drafting of the Appeal. A fourth, Charles Gore, had addressed the drafting committee.[75]

---

73 Report of Gailor's sermon in *The Times*, 9 August 1920, p. 7, col. A. See also "Lambeth 1920" (ed. Methuen), 529.

74 "Lambeth 1920" (ed. Methuen), 529–531, citing *The Times*, 21 August 1920; p. 4, col B (Stafford) and 17 August 1920, 6, col. C (MacFadyen).

75 The 14 Anglican bishops with Brent were Cecil Henry Boutflower (South Tokyo), Edward Arthur Dunn (British Honduras with Central America), John Cragg Farthing (Montreal), Charles Gore (retired Bishop

The Archbishop of Canterbury sent the Appeal not only to all provinces of the Anglican Communion, but to churches around the world, eliciting mostly positive resolutions and responses from the Church of Scotland and the Free Church of Scotland, the Baptist Union, the Presbyterian Church of England, the Congregational Union, the Wesleyan Methodist Church, the Primitive Methodist Church, the United Methodist Church, and the Moravian Church.[76] He also received an invitation from the Church of Sweden for an

of Oxford), John Allen Fitzgerald Gregg (Ossory, Ferns and Leighlin), John McKim (Bishop of Tokyo), James Okey Nash (Coadjutor, Cape Town), Jervois Arthur Newnham (Saskatchewan), Francis Lushington Norris (North China), Edwin James Palmer (Bombay), Charles Edward Plumb (St. Andrews), Gilbert White (Willochra), David Williams (Huron), Joseph Watkin Williams (St. John's South Africa). In total 136 delegates are included in the list of attendees, including one woman. See World Conference on Faith and Order, *Report of the Preliminary Meeting held at Geneva, Switzerland August 12-20, 1920* (n.p.: Continuation Committee, 1920), 2-15.

76 The file of notifications and responses includes correspondence pertaining to the Appeal with Cardinal Bourne and other leaders of the Roman Catholic Church, the Orthodox Eastern Church, the Armenian and Georgian Churches, the Church of Sweden, the Church of Scotland and United Free Church of Scotland, the Evangelical Free Churches in England, the Baptist Union and the Presbyterian Church of England, the Congregational Union, the Wesleyan Methodist Church, the Primitive Methodist Church, the United Methodist Church, the Moravian Church, the Pan-Presbyterian Council, the Federal Council of Evangelical Free Churches of England, the General Body of Protestant Dissenting Ministers (Presbyterian, Independent, Baptist), the Presbyterian Church of New Zealand, and the Kikuyu Alliance of Missionary Societies: see LPL Davidson Papers, vol. 268. These responses would be worthy of further study.

Anglican bishop or bishops to participate in an episcopal consecration on 19 September 1920,[77] which Hensley Henson as Bishop of Durham duly did.[78] In October 1920, the Archbishop of Canterbury reported to the Primus of the Church of Scotland: "I am giving many Addresses about the Lambeth Conference and am urging everywhere the need of patience and the mischief of imagining that

---

77 Telegram from the Church of Sweden, in LPL Davidson Papers, vol. 268, fol. 10. This was not just a response to the Appeal but also to Lambeth 1920 Resolutions 24 and 25: "24. The Conference welcomes the Report of the Commission appointed after the last Conference entitled 'The Church of England and the Church of Sweden,' and, accepting the conclusions there maintained on the succession of bishops of the Church of Sweden and the conception of the priesthood set forth in its standards, recommends that members of that Church, qualified to receive the sacrament in their own Church, should be admitted to Holy Communion in ours. It also recommends that on suitable occasions permission should be given to Swedish ecclesiastics to give addresses in our churches. 25. We recommend further that in the event of an invitation being extended to an Anglican bishop or bishops to take part in the consecration of a Swedish bishop, the invitation should, if possible, be accepted, subject to the approval of the metropolitan. We also recommend that, in the first instance, as an evident token of the restoration of closer relations between the two Churches, if possible more than one of our bishops should take part in the consecration."

78 Herbert Hensley Henson, *Retrospective of an Unimportant Life* (Oxford: Oxford University Press, 1942), vol. 1, 321. In May 1920, Henson had received from Archbishop Söderblom "an invitation to 'assist' at the consecration of two diocesan Swedish bishops" the following September, which he had immediately accepted, only subsequently informing the Archbishop of Canterbury, who "at first expressed satisfaction, then incertitude." See Henson, *Retrospective of an Unimportant Life*, vol. 1, 319-320.

we have short cuts to a solution."[79]

However, not all the responses were positive. In Scotland, Norman Maclean published an article on the Appeal entitled: "The Two Voices: Peace, peace, where there is no peace," in which he complained that "the Lambeth Appeal speaks with two voices, and the one negates the other."[80] He wrote to the Bishop of Barrow: "Nobody could have approved the Lambeth proposals with greater sympathy or expectation. My disappointment was in proportion to my hopes."[81] MacLean was particularly exercised by the provision restricting admission to Communion:

> The clauses that utterly destroy all hope so far as we are concerned are those regarding admission to the Holy Communion. I have never met any Church of Scotland minister who wanted to officiate at your altars. But if we belong to the One Lord then we should come together at our Lord's table. But this you term an 'irregularity.' I have always deemed it a privilege to receive the Holy Communion in the parish churches of England when South of the Border. I feel it keenly that I shall never again be able to have that privilege. I could not come to the Holy Table under the conditions of 'Irregularity' as now defined. No proposals for Church Union

79 Archbishop of Canterbury to the Primus of the Scottish Episcopal Church, 23 October 1920, LPL Davidson Papers, vol. 266, fol. 31.

80 *Glasgow Herald* 28.09.1920.

81 Norman MacLean to the Bishop of Barrow, 8 October 1920, LPL Lang Papers, vol. 59, fol. 64r.

can possibly come to fruition that are tainted & in spirits so alien as this is to the Christian ideal.[82]

In contrast James Cooper, Professor of Ecclesiastical History at the University of Glasgow, and a committed ecumenist who had been present at the Faith and Order meeting in Geneva, affirmed to Lang: "I had some thoughts of offering myself up for ordination—on the Lambeth conditions—but think it better to wait a little, and try to get the Assembly's assent to several of us doing so—remaining, of course, ministers of the Church of Scotland."[83] In the event, although the 1922 General Assembly of the Church of Scotland affirmed that the Appeal "may be regarded as one of the most important of the many recent expressions of the spirit of reconciliation for which we have cause to give thanks to God,"[84] negotiations relating to the reunion of the Church of Scotland and the United Free Church took precedence.

In England, the Appeal led to a long period of negotiations between the Church of England and the English Free Churches. A "Memorandum on the status on nonconformist ministers" in the papers of Arthur Cayley Headlam, Bishop of Gloucester, laid out

---

82 Norman MacLean to the Bishop of Barrow, 8 October 1920, LPL Lang Papers, vol. 59, fol. 64r, fol. 65v.

83 James Cooper to Lang, 6 October 1920, LPL Lang Papers, vol. 59, fol. 63r. Cooper described himself as "an advocate of Christian unity since his college days": Faith and Order, *Report of the Preliminary Meeting at Switzerland August 12–20, 1920*, 5.

84 General Assembly of the Church of Scotland, *Report of Committee on Church and Nation*, 24 May 1922, "Lambeth Proposals," in LPL Davidson Papers, vol. 266, fol. 165.

principles for negotiating the relationship, the second and third of which came to characterise the Church of England's involvement in Meißen-type ecumenical agreements in the 1980s:

1. There should be no reordination. It should be recognised that whatever defects either side may find in the orders of the other are obliterated by the formal recognition of reunion. Whether there should be a solemn service in which this mutual recognition was accomplished and what if it were held should be its character is a question that may be postponed.

2. This Reunion should imply the removal of any bar to intercommunion. It should remove any bar to preaching in one another's pulpits and should mean reunion in synods and other representative bodies.

3. Reunion would not imply any right of intercelebration. The ministers of each reunited church would continue to celebrate in their own churches and according to their own rites and usages.

4. All ordinations after reunion should be such as satisfy the regulations of all the bodies uniting. All ordinations would be by bishops, but the ministers of other bodies should take part in the laying on of hands.[85]

The memorandum also pointed out: "It was really just as difficult for Augustine to recognise Donatist orders as it is for an English High Churchman to recognise Presbyterian orders."[86] Be that as it may, the Anglican protagonists underestimated the sense of many Free Church

85 *Ibid.*, fol. 58-60 (pp. 7-9).

86 LPL Headlam papers MS 2629 fol. 55 (p. 4).

ministers that, despite the rhetoric of the Lambeth Appeal, their ministries-to-date were not being affirmed. These concerns about ordination, already lodged in the ecumenical movement before the Lambeth Appeal, led to the failure of the dialogue.

CONCLUSION

This article has shown that the 1920 Appeal to All Christian People drew on and interacted with a wide range of Anglican ecumenical initiatives of the period. Engaging with the same theological questions and the same tensions around episcopacy, it took a middle line on the question of engagement with non-episcopal churches. As the most feted resolution of a landmark Lambeth Conference, the Appeal framed and motivated Anglican ecumenical thinking throughout the interwar period, setting the stage for Anglican ecclesiology thereafter.

TWO

The Vision of the Appeal to All Christian People

John Bauerschmidt

The "Appeal to All Christian People" issued by the 1920 Lambeth Conference is a most significant document of the modern Ecumenical Movement. It was certainly one of the most compelling statements in the early days of the movement that had begun a decade before with the 1910 World Missionary Conference in Edinburgh. The issuing of the Appeal is also arguably the single most significant action of any Lambeth Conference. In terms of Lambeth Conference texts, the 1948 statement on the dispersed nature of authority in Anglicanism, contained in a committee report on the Anglican Communion, is perhaps better known, or at least more widely quoted by ecclesiologists.[1] In terms of actions, the 1930 Conference Resolution 15 dealing with contraception is often referred to as significant, in terms of Christian grappling with issues of ethics in the pre-dawn period of the sexual revolution.[2]

Yet the Appeal still figures most prominently, as text and action, both in terms of the Ecumenical Movement and in terms of Anglicanism itself. The bishops were conscious of the power of the Holy Spirit, the "rushing mighty wind" of Acts 2:2 that several called to mind in their accounts.[3] The Appeal was a rousing call to action addressed to people, not churches; a call for the reunion of the Church Catholic. It was the product of an extraordinary gathering of Anglican leaders with outstanding gifts, representing many constituencies, held at an auspicious moment—in the shadow of the Great War and in the context of a great missionary expansion of Anglicanism. The Appeal met with objections generated by churchmanship and modernism, but managed nonetheless to create something fresh and new, of enduring influence.

---

1   *The Lambeth Conference 1948: The Encyclical Letter from the Bishops; Together with Resolutions and Reports (London: SPCK, 1948), II.85. See John Bauerschmidt, "Architecture of Authority" in When Churches in Communion Disagree, ed. Robert Heaney, Christopher Wells, and Pierre Whalon (Dallas: Living Church Books, 2022).*

2   *The Lambeth Conference 1930: Encyclical Letter from the Bishops with Resolutions and Reports (London: SPCK, 1930), 43.*

3   Cosmo Gordan Lang in a letter to Wilfred Parker immediately after the Conference, quoted in J.G. Lockhart, *Cosmo Gordon Lang (London: Hodder and Stoughton), 270. Lang attributed this description to Neville Talbot, Bishop of Pretoria. See also* Frank Theodore Woods, Frank Weston, and Martin Linton Smith, *Lambeth and Reunion (London: SPCK, 1921), 53.*

I will focus here on the text of the 1920 Appeal and identify some themes, taking as a broad framework the substantial scriptural note contained in the Appeal, in the middle of Section IV: "Forgetting the things behind and reaching out to the goal." This is an allusion to Philippians 3:13, a text that St. Augustine deployed most famously in the *Confessions*, in his account of the vision shared by him and his mother Monica in Ostia. Here the bishops deploy it in their own vision of a reunited Church, capable of moving beyond the barriers of past division to a hoped-for future. In ecumenical literature, the text appears again in the Common Declaration of Archbishop Michael Ramsey and Pope Paul VI in 1966, recalled by Archbishop Welby and Pope Francis in their own Common Declaration of 2016.[4]

The Appeal does not stand by itself but must be considered in relation to several other documents produced by the conference. First, there is the encyclical letter, addressed to the faithful, issued by the bishops at the close of the gathering: a standard feature of earlier Lambeth Conferences. Reunion figured, first and foremost, in the matters taken up in the encyclical, which in its structure and diverse subject matter mirrored the work done by the committees of the conference. The organizing idea of the encyclical, however, was "fellowship": a subject that Randall Davidson, Archbishop of Canterbury and president of the conference, intended should be emphasized.[5]

---

4 "Common Declaration by Pope Paul VI and the Archbishop of Canterbury Dr. Michael Ramsey" (24 March 1966) and "Common Declaration of His Holiness Pope Francis and His Grace Justin Welby Archbishop of Canterbury" (5 Oct. 2016), both available online.

5 G.K.A. Bell, *Randall Davidson,* 2nd edn. (London: OUP, 1938), 1015.

Second, there are the conference committee reports, the result of the deliberations of the committees outside of plenary session. The "Committee Appointed to Consider Relation to and Reunion with Other Churches," the so-called Reunion Committee, produced a report that was received by the conference, but which did not have the same standing as the encyclical letter or resolutions.[6] The Reunion Committee did its work in two sub-committees, one concerned with other episcopal churches and the other with non-episcopal churches. Each of these sub-committees also produced a report: a fairly short one in the case of the former, and a longer one in the latter.

The Appeal itself was adopted as Resolution 9 by the conference, but it also passed other closely related resolutions that bore on reunion, Resolutions 10-16. These resolutions were collected together in a group after the Appeal in the published proceedings, but the separate reports of the committees make clear that three of the resolutions (10, 14, 15) were the result of the recommendations of the committee as a whole, while the other four (11-13, 16) are found in the separate report of the sub-committee on non-episcopal churches. This includes the important Resolution 12.

We know that this sub-committee, with its large number of members, did a good deal of the work on reunion, including generating the Appeal.[7] Cosmo Gordon Lang, the Archbishop of York,

---

6 *Conference of Bishops of the Anglican Communion: Holden at Lambeth Palace, July 5 to August 7, 1920 (London: SPCK, 1920), 23.*

7 See "Lambeth 1920: The Appeal to All Christian People—An account by G. K. A. Bell and the redactions of the Appeal," ed. Charlotte Methuen, in Melanie Barber, Gabriel Sewell and Stephen Taylor, ed., *From the Reformation to the Permissive Society: A Miscellany in Celebration of the*

chaired both the Reunion Committee and the sub-committee; Edwin James Palmer, the Bishop of Bombay, acted as one of the secretaries of both groups, as well as the drafter of the encyclical at the end. The Archbishop of Canterbury frequented the Reunion Committee's sessions, and his chaplain and biographer, George Bell, also attended its sessions and the after-hours work of various drafting groups commissioned by the sub-committee.[8] The much smaller sub-committee on episcopal churches was the source of Resolutions 17–31, which mostly dealt with the reception of reports on the relations of the Communion with other episcopal bodies, expressions of support for embattled episcopal churches, and the monitoring and extension of continuing relationships. These resolutions were peripheral to the Appeal, though concern for unity with other episcopal churches was well represented in the members of the Conference and left its stamp on the Appeal itself.

❋ ❋ ❋

A prominent note of the Appeal is that of penitence, which appears as emblematic of the "forgetting of things behind" of Phil. 3:13. This emphasis was remarked upon by participants at the time, and afterwards in retrospect.[9] The bishops sounded this note in the opening

---

400th Anniversary of Lambeth Palace Library (Woodbridge, UK: Boydell & Brewer, 2010), 527.

8 Bell, *Randall Davidson,* 1011; Methuen, "Lambeth 1920," 526.

9 Woods et al., *Lambeth and Reunion,* 48; Thomas Frank Gailor, "The Lambeth Committee on Reunion," *The Constructive Quarterly* 8 (1920), 537-9; Bell,

of the Appeal. "We believe that the Holy Spirit has called us in a very solemn and special manner to associate ourselves in penitence and prayer with all those who deplore the divisions of Christian people, and are inspired by the vision and hope of a visible unity of the whole Church" (Appeal, §III). The "forgetting of things behind," when it appears in Section IV, serves in fact to summarize the previous three sections, with their acknowledgment of the fact of division and analysis of its causes:

> The causes of division lie deep in the past, and are by no means simple or wholly blameworthy, Yet none can doubt that self-will, ambition, and lack of charity among Christians have been principal factors in the mingled process, and that these, together with blindness to the sin of disunion, are still mainly responsible for the breaches of Christendom. We acknowledge this condition of broken fellowship to be contrary to God's will, and we desire frankly to confess our share in the guilt of thus crippling the Body of Christ and hindering the activity of His Spirit. (Appeal, §III)

This emphasis on the need for penitence and confession of complicity in the sin of disunion may seem like a commonplace of ecumenical work today, but that is no doubt a tribute in part to the influence of the Appeal.

※ ※ ※

Randall Davidson, 1012.

The emphasis on penitence serves to highlight and to point forward to what is the singular theme of the Conference, found most substantially in the encyclical but also here in the Appeal. "We believe that God wills fellowship": the statement lies at the beginning of Section I, and entered the process with a second draft prepared by a small working group of bishops, commissioned after a conversation between the Archbishop of Canterbury and George Bell.[10] Sin breaks fellowship: hence the need for repentance. The theme of fellowship, however, had been present in the first draft or statement presented earlier in committee by the Archbishop of York, but without this brilliant organizing summation.[11]

The words drawn from the beginning of the Appeal are memorable ones, but we should not lose sight of the more extensive treatment of the theme in the encyclical letter, issued at the end of the Conference. George Bell provides a memorable scene in his diary of the man his wife called "Jimmy Bombay," sitting on the ground cross-legged, at work in the "Encyclical circle."[12] Bell considered the Bishop of Bombay to have dealt fairly freely with the draft sections contributed by others in favor of his own formulations.[13] The relationship between the Appeal and the encyclical was not linear, of course, and we can assume cross-fertilization that was fairly continuous and ran both ways.

10 Charlotte Methuen, "The Making of 'An Appeal to All Christian People'" in *The Lambeth Conference: Theology, Polity, and Purpose*, ed. Paul Avis and Benjamin M. Guyer (London: T&T Clark, 2017), 121.

11 Methuen, "Making," 119.

12 Ronald C.D. Jasper, *George Bell (London: OUP, 1967)*, 57.

13 Methuen, "Lambeth 1920," 541.

The encyclical makes clear that with "fellowship" the bishops were commending and adopting as their main theme not a generalized notion of human kinship or relationship but rather fellowship in the Pauline sense of 2 Cor. 13:14. The theological ground for its deployment was well prepared in the encyclical, with its acknowledgment that "primacy belongs to the order of creation,"[14] the relationship that exists between God and humanity and between human beings themselves by virtue of their creation in the image of God. The encyclical then continues:

> He chose a nation, and made it in a special sense His own, that within it love of God and men might be cultivated, and that thus it might enlighten the world. Into that nation He sent forth His Son, both to reconcile the world to Himself and to reconcile men one to another. And His Son formed a new and greater Israel, which we call the Church, to carry on His own mission of reconciling men to God and men to men. The foundation and ground of all fellowship is the undeflected will of God, renewing again and again its patient effort to possess, without destroying, the wills of men. And so He has called into being a fellowship of men, His Church, and sent His Holy Spirit to abide therein, that by the prevailing attraction of that one Spirit, He, the one God and Father of all, may win over the whole human family to that one fellowship in Himself, by which alone it can attain to the fulness of life. This then is the object of

---

14 "Encyclical Letter," in *Conference of Bishops, 10.*

the Church.... [I]n order to accomplish its object, the Church must itself be a pattern of fellowship.[15]

The close theological connection between the encyclical and the Appeal here is clear. The Appeal takes up the common theme in its first section:

> We believe that God wills fellowship. By God's own act this fellowship was made in and through Jesus Christ, and its life is in his Spirit. We believe that it is God's purpose to manifest this fellowship, so far as this world is concerned, in an outward, visible, and united society, holding one faith, having its own recognized officers, using God-given means of grace, and inspiring all its members to the world-wide service of the Kingdom of God. This is what we mean by the Catholic Church. (Appeal, §I)

In linking the notion of fellowship to the visible Church, and casting fellowship both in terms of character and vocation, the encyclical and Appeal anticipate, *avant la lettre*, the "communion ecclesiology" of a later period.[16]

Yet the Appeal goes on to claim that "this united fellowship is not visible in the world to-day." The churches are divided: the "ancient episcopal Communions" of East and West, and the "great non-episcopal Communions" as well (Appeal, §II).The Catholic Church exists,

---

15 "Encyclical Letter," 10-11.

16 Ephraim Radner, "Christian Mission and the Lambeth Conferences," in *Lambeth Conference, ed. Avis and Guyer, 148.*

as present reality, yet its unity remains to be manifested.

For this reason, in Section IV, the Appeal, tracking with Philippians 3:13, begins to reach forward to what lies ahead: "The times call us to a new outlook and new measures.... The time has come, we believe, for all the separated groups of Christians to agree in forgetting the things which are behind and reaching out towards the goal of a reunited Catholic Church" (Appeal, §IV). This will mean, the text continues, "an adventure of goodwill and still more of faith, for nothing less is required than a new discovery of the creative resources of God. To this adventure we are convinced that God is now calling the members of His Church" (Appeal, §V).

※ ※ ※

To the prominent notes of penitence and fellowship in the Appeal we should add the notion of gifts possessed by the Church. The Appeal alludes to these twice. First, in Section II, the mention of the gifts possessed by the different communions within the divided Church is alluded to, with a note both of celebration and of regret: "We are all organized in different groups, each one keeping to itself gifts that rightly belong to the whole fellowship, and tending to live its own life apart from the rest" (Appeal, §II). Then again, in Section IV, the gifts take their proper place within the reunited fellowship:

> The vision which rises before us is that of a Church, genuinely Catholic, loyal to all Truth, and gathering into its fellowship all "who profess and call themselves Christians," within whose visible unity all the treasures of faith and order, bequeathed as a heritage by

the past to the present, shall be possessed in common, and made serviceable to the Whole Body of Christ. Within this unity Christian Communions now separated from one another would retain much that has long been distinctive in their methods of worship and service. It is through a rich diversity of life and devotion that the unity of the whole fellowship will be fulfilled. (Appeal, §II)

The acknowledgment of a diversity of gifts creates an argument for the necessity of sharing them. Here we find another fruitful theme of the ecumenical movement: the notion of different gifts that must be received within the whole fellowship.[17]

There is another scriptural allusion in the Appeal's discussion of gifts that should not be lost sight of, for it colors any consideration of the positive value of the divisions that exist between Christians. The echo here of the withholding of Ananias and Sapphira from the church in Jerusalem, recounted in Acts 5:1-11, works against any valorization of division on account of the gifts generated thereby. These gifts in their diversity properly belong to the fellowship, according to the Appeal, and not to the divided churches themselves.

※ ※ ※

A final aspect of the Appeal remains to be considered, namely, the re-statement of the Chicago-Lambeth Quadrilateral that occupies

---

17 See the Third Anglican-Roman Catholic International Commission (ARCIC III), *Walking Together on the Way: Learning to Be the Church—Local, Regional, Universal* (London: SPCK, 2018), 15.

a large part of the whole. Alongside this, we may place the critical Resolution 12, in which the bishops attempted to hedge around the work done in the Appeal, and to provide guidance to the churches of the Communion.

The story of the Quadrilateral is well-known.[18] Emerging from the work of the American priest William Reed Huntington, adopted by the House of Bishops of the Protestant Episcopal Church in 1886, and then by the 1888 Lambeth Conference as "Articles" that supplied "a basis on which approach may be by God's blessing made toward Home Reunion,"[19] this Quadrilateral had been reaffirmed by Lambeth Conferences in the intervening years as the formula for the reunion of the Church. The Holy Scriptures of the Old and New Testament; the Apostles' and Nicene Creeds; the Sacraments of Baptism and the Supper of the Lord; and the "Historic Episcopate, locally adapted in the methods of its administration to the varying needs of the nations and peoples called of God into the Unity of His Church."[20]

In calling for progress toward the vision of reunion embraced by the conference, the Appeal deployed the Quadrilateral, but not without a distinction. In Section VI the Appeal states that "the visible unity of the Church will be found to involve the wholehearted acceptance of" four items. Scriptures, Creeds, and Sacraments find a place, now couched within the terms of fellowship. For the fourth

18   See J. Robert Wright, "Heritage and Vision: The Chicago-Lambeth Quadrilateral," in *Quadrilateral at One Hundred (Cincinnati, Ohio: Forward Movement, 1988), 8-46.*

19   1979 Book of Common Prayer, 877.

20   *Ibid., 878.*

and final note, the Appeal then calls for "a ministry acknowledged by every part of the Church as possessing not only the inward call of the Spirit, but also the commission of Christ and the authority of the whole body" (Appeal, §VI).

Almost without a breath, the Appeal then goes on in the following section, in the very next sentence, to restore with the second hand what the first hand had seemingly removed. "May we not reasonably claim that the Episcopate is the one means of providing such a ministry?" (Appeal, §VII). Section VII goes on to acknowledge that non-episcopal ministries have been "effective means of grace," but then argues that both history and present experience uphold the bishops' claim regarding the episcopate. The Appeal adds that the future will show that the episcopate is the "best instrument for maintaining the unity and continuity of the Church" (Appeal, §VII). Here we touch the world of the 1982 Lima Document, *Baptism, Eucharist, and Ministry*, perhaps by adding that the episcopate, if it is the best instrument, is not the only one.[21]

Even a commendation of the "apostolic rite of the laying on of hands" (that is, confirmation by the bishop) makes it into Section VII, a sign of the careful negotiation between church parties that was taking place at the Conference. That it was not demanded as a prerequisite of unity is a sign that Anglo-Catholics had given something in the Appeal. That it was included at all is a reminder of their influence, as well as the sincere attachment of Anglicans of all sorts

---

21 World Council of Churches' Commission on Faith and Order, *Baptism, Eucharist and Ministry, Faith and Order Paper no. 111, 1982; available online.*

to episcopal confirmation.[22]

The mention of confirmation enters the text with a third draft, as does the word "reasonably."[23] This word is worth acknowledging, because it seems to soften the claim made on behalf of the episcopate, while at the same time couching the Appeal within the theological method often identified with Richard Hooker. Reason serves here, as it did in the time of Hooker, as an ordering principal that brings coherence, not as a critical tool that discerns difference, and is admirably deployed by the Appeal. What seems to be a softening of the claims of the Appeal really functions as a strengthening argument for taking up its challenge, in the name of a hoped-for order susceptible of reasoned explanation in aid of furthering the coherence of the churches.

Then Section VIII makes the Appeal's chief offer:

> We believe that for all, the truly equitable approach to union is by way of mutual deference to one another's consciences. To this end, we who send forth this appeal would say that if the authorities of other Communions should so desire, we are persuaded that, terms of union having been otherwise satisfactorily adjusted, bishops and clergy of our Communion would willingly accept from these authorities a form of commission or recognition which would commend our ministry to their congregations, as having its place in the one family life. (Appeal, §VIII)

---

22 See F.L. Cross, *Darwell Stone (Westminster, UK: Dacre Press, 1943)*, 140-147, for an account of the reaction of Stone, the Principal of Pusey House, Oxford, and other Anglo-Catholics, to the 1920 Lambeth Appeal.

23 Methuen, "Lambeth 1920."

This offer was interpreted by Frank Weston, the Bishop of Zanzibar, but also by others, as chiefly applying to a reconciliation of ministries with the episcopal churches of East and West, in particular the Church of Rome, which would most likely insist on reordination of Anglican ministers.[24] For Anglo-Catholics, the Appeal promised to move Anglicans beyond the impasse of Roman denial of the validity of Anglican Orders, sparking the Malines Conversations with Cardinal Mercier initiated by Lord Halifax in 1921.[25]

Weston is given credit by George Bell and others for having made a substantial contribution to the Appeal, chiefly in supporting it and thereby providing cover for other bishops of the Catholic party.[26] Weston was responsible for the idea of the different Communions as each constituting a "group" within the one *Catholica*.[27] This approximates to the Appeal's call for a Church reunited rather than any one Communion absorbed by another (see Appeal, §IX). To some extent, the sub-committee on non-episcopal churches waited at the beginning of each session to see if the Bishop of Zanzibar had thought better of what he had said supporting the Appeal at the previous session! Bell writes in his biography of Randall Davidson that Weston had "an extraordinary mixture of generosity and menace"[28]—clearly driven by the uncertainty he generated.

---

24 Woods et al., *Lambeth and Reunion*, 60.

25 Bell, *Randall Davidson, 1256*.

26 Bell, *Randall Davidson, 1012*.

27 Methuen, "Lambeth 1920," 537. See also Wood, Weston, and Smith, 62, where it is called "the Lambeth Conference's group theory."

28 Bell, 1010.

Yet the framing of Resolution 12 was probably the most significant contribution of Weston to the process. Though his draft was modified, it did form the basis of the compromise that Resolution 12 represented.[29] The Resolution is couched in terms of counsel that the conference was prepared to offer to the bishops, clergy, and members of the Church in implementing the call to reunion.

First, counsel in regard to "prospects and projects of reunion."[30] The move toward reunion having been agreed between churches, a bishop might allow non-episcopally ordained ministers who had embraced the ideals of the Appeal to preach in his diocese. Moreover, bishops would not be subject to questions if "in the few years between the initiation and completion of a definite scheme of union" the bishop admitted to communion baptized but unconfirmed communicants of non-episcopal congregations.[31] Then: a general provision endorsing the sub-committee's report, which implicitly gave the churches of the Communion latitude in dealing with the remaining non-episcopally ordained ministers in the period after union, while ensuring that episcopal churches were served by episcopal ministers. The Appeal, significantly, had not insisted that all ministers must be episcopally ordained before union. Rather: "It is our hope that the same motive would lead ministers who have not received it to accept a commission through episcopal ordination, as obtaining for them a ministry throughout the whole fellowship" (Appeal, §VIII).

29 Methuen, "Making," 564.

30 "Resolution 12" in *Conference of Bishops of the Anglican Communion, 30; available online.*

31 *Ibid.*

Second, counsel as to what actions ought to be avoided in seeking reunion. "General schemes of intercommunion or exchange of pulpits" could not be countenanced.[32] In addition, the conference could not approve of the celebration of Holy Communion in Anglican churches for Anglicans by non-episcopally ordained ministers.

Third, counsel as to doubtful matters. The rule of the necessity of confirmation before receiving communion was not to be interpreted to exclude baptized but unconfirmed members of other churches who desired to receive communion "under conditions which in the Bishop's judgement justified their admission" (Appeal, §IX). Where that permission could not be obtained beforehand, the priest was reminded that he had no canonical authority to repel a communicant for any other reasons than those spelled out in the rubrics at the end of the Communion office.

※ ※ ※

To my mind, Resolution 12 serves the valuable purpose of creating a theological space for the issuing of a broad-based Appeal that is intended for diverse audiences. It attempts to articulate a common position while also allowing the churches of the Communion to address different contexts as they pursued reunion. A key formulation, both in the Appeal and in Resolution 12, was the prior agreement on the principles of reunion found in the Appeal. This agreement created room for latitude in practice in the present, in view of agreed practice in the future. These resolutions are in some sense limited to

32   *Ibid.*

their own time, yet they have been useful in ecumenical agreements over the years.

The 1920 Lambeth Appeal created a new environment for the fledgling Ecumenical Movement. By emphasizing the idea of fellowship, it capitalized on post-war movements within the broader culture and claimed this ground for specifically Christian reflection, while also anticipating broader theological reflection on the theme of communion. Using the rallying cry of Philippians 3:13, it held up a vision that allowed the divided churches to begin "to agree in forgetting the things which are behind and reaching out towards the goal of a reunited Catholic Church." In a framework of repentance, it challenged the members of the churches to consider the sacrifices they were prepared to make "for the sake of a common fellowship, a common ministry, and a common service to the world" (Appeal, §IX). It encouraged the churches to see their diverse gifts as the common possession of the one *Catholica*, rather than as gifts to be kept to themselves. The Appeal remains of lasting significance for ecumenists, ecclesiologists, and church leaders as they continue the work of Christian union in a new century.

THREE

Seeking Unity, Increasing Tensions

The Church of South India and the Appeal

Jeremy Worthen

SETTING THE STAGE

One of the remarkable things about the "Appeal to all Christian People" issued by the Lambeth Conference of 1920 was that it managed to secure such widespread support at the time. Only four of the bishops present failed to approve the text in the final vote. Those who had shaped it were relieved that the Anglican Communion could speak with one voice on this subject. The Archbishop of York, Cosmo Gordon Lang, who chaired the Reunion Committee that proposed the Appeal to the conference as a whole, had written to a trusted friend beforehand that "I have a Committee of more than 60 Bishops to deal with, containing every variety of opinion, from Zanzibar and Nassau to Durham, and my heart fails me when I think of the difficulties." In looking back afterwards on the harmonious outcome, "it was difficult—for me impossible—to think that this wind was other than the wind of the Spirit."[1] He and the others who had drafted the text were well aware of the difficulty of composing words about unity around which Anglicans could unite.[2]

In 1920, unity was known to be a subject that could polarise the Anglican Communion. The Kikuyu controversy in the preceding

---

1   "Lambeth 1920: The Appeal to All Christian People: An Account by G. K. A. Bell and the Redactions of the Appeal," ed. Charlotte Methuen, in *From the Reformation to the Permissive Society: A Miscellany in Celebration of the 400th Anniversary of Lambeth Palace Library*, ed. Melanie Barber and Stephen Taylor with Gabriel Sewell, Church of England Record Society vol. 18 (Woodbridge, Suffolk: Boydell, 2010), 529-31. For the quotations from Lang, see Methuen's more recent article, "The Making of 'An Appeal to All Christian People' at the 1920 Lambeth Conference," in *The Lambeth Conference: Theology, History, Polity and Purpose*, ed. Paul Avis and Benjamin Guyer (London: Bloomsbury T&T Clark, 2017), 116 and 128. For a more sober assessment of what was achieved, from the perspective of the then Archbishop of Canterbury, see Michael Hughes, *Archbishop Randall Davidson* (London: Routledge, 2018), 112-15, and 209-10.

2   For a full collection of the documents of the 1920 Lambeth Conference, see Randall Davidson, ed., *The Six Lambeth Conferences 1867–1920* (London: SPCK, 1929). The Resolutions from all Lambeth Conferences, including the text of the Lambeth Appeal as Resolution 9, are available on the Anglican Communion website. The report on "Relation to and Reunion with Other Churches" notes disagreements within the committee about the wording of some Resolutions (143).

decade had demonstrated the sharply different approaches within Anglicanism to relations with other churches. Given the leading role of the Bishop of Zanzibar, Frank Weston, in that controversy, it was not surprising that his presence on the Reunion Committee in 1920 caused Lang a good deal of anxiety at the outset. To some extent, the contrasting views were associated with the two major Church of England missionary societies, the Church Missionary Society (CMS) and the Society for the Propagation of the Gospel (SPG), whose work was inseparable from the formation of the Anglican Communion. While the former was broadly supportive of emerging initiatives for closer partnership with Protestant churches, an SPG publication in 1915 asserted that "Union between the Anglican Church and the great Protestant denominations in religious teaching and life does not make for real union. It splits the church into fragments and puts off the day of real union."[3] Supporters of SPG were not against unity, but some tended to look to Rome and the Orthodox Churches as their controlling horizon. Anything Anglicans did that might diminish their claim to have maintained the Catholic order of the first millennium could only undermine the ecumenical vocation of Anglicanism in their eyes.

In the decade before the Lambeth Appeal was made, similar issues around Anglican engagement with initiatives for unity were also evident in India. Here too, such initiatives were powerfully motivated by the common desire in all churches to seize the opportunities for evangelization that were perceived to be opening up. The 1910

3 Quoted in Bengt Sundkler, *Church of South India: The Movement Towards Union 1900-1947* (London: Lutterworth Press, 1954), 76.

World Missionary Conference in Edinburgh had been significant for many in underscoring the intrinsic relationship between mission and unity.[4] Running alongside this, there was also a concern to overcome the perception that Christianity with its competing identities deriving from Western European history must remain a stranger to emerging Indian national consciousness. The Church of England in India had its first Indian bishop in 1912 with the consecration of Samuel Azariah, who had made a noteworthy contribution at the World Missionary Conference two years earlier,[5] and moves initiated soon afterwards eventually led to the establishment in 1927 of the Church of India, Burma and Ceylon as an autonomous Province of the Anglican Communion. While such developments were certainly welcomed, many felt strongly that the desire for union could not be put off, as national aspirations grew stronger: "genuine indigenization in India was perceived to require the effacement of ecclesial divisions inherited from the missionary Churches and societies of the West."[6]

In this context, a consensus can be seen developing in the first two decades of the twentieth century between Anglican leaders in India from the CMS and SPG wings on the importance of visible unity and how it might be achieved, a consensus that anticipates the position of

---

4 Brian Stanley, *The World Missionary Conference, Edinburgh 1910*, Studies in the History of Christian Missions (Grand Rapids, Michigan: Eerdmans, 2009); Sundkler, *Church of South India*, 61-70.

5 Stanley, *World Missionary Conference*, 121-28.

6 Titus Presler, "Witness, Advocacy and Union: Anglicanism's Twentieth-Century Contribution to Minority Christianity in South Asia" in *The Oxford History of Anglicanism*, vol. V: *Global Anglicanism, c. 1910-2000*, ed. William L. Sachs (Oxford: Oxford University Press, 2018), 400.

the Lambeth Appeal in significant ways.[7] Dialogue between Indian representatives of the Anglican Church and the South India United Church (formed from former Presbyterian and Congregationalist churches) led to the publication in 1919 of what became known as the Tranquebar Manifesto, resting on "this common ground of the historic Episcopate and of spiritual equality of all members of the two Churches."[8] That twofold emphasis corresponds closely to the territory mapped out a year later at the Lambeth Conference. The role of the Bishop of Bombay, E. J. Palmer—who had been a key figure in discussions about union in India over the preceding decade—as secretary to Lang's Reunion Committee in 1920 is hardly coincidental. Nonetheless, there was a sense for those closely involved in the South India proposals that the Lambeth Appeal ultimately represented a failure to embrace the path they had pioneered as fully as they would have had hoped.[9]

Over the next two decades, the developing proposals for the churches in South India remained one of the most prominent examples of attempts within the Anglican Communion to realise the vision of the Lambeth Appeal by seeking a union of churches in one place that would make visible the unity that expresses God's will for fellowship. In 1930, the encyclical letter to accompany circulation of

---

7 Sundkler, *Church of South India*, 62-72.

8 For the full text, see Sundkler, *Church of South India*, 101-3. It also appears under the heading of the "South India Proposals for Christian Union—South India United Church and the Anglican Church" in G. K. A. Bell, ed., *Documents Bearing on the Problem of Christian Unity and Fellowship 1916-1920* (London: SPCK, 1920), 26-28.

9 Sundkler, *Church of South India*, 131-35.

the Lambeth Conference documents compared the "holy aspirations" of ten years earlier with the "God-guided actions" that had followed from them, singling out "the scheme for a union of Churches in South India, which... has now reached an advanced stage" as one example, alongside dialogues with the Old Catholics and the Orthodox.[10] Still, there were also indications that clouds had already appeared in the sky:

> This process cannot be initiated without sacrifices, and must in its early stages involve anomalies and irregularities—a prospect which gives rise to serious misgivings in many minds. But these misgivings are outweighed by hope and by our trust in God's will to perfect His work of reconciliation.... We feel that in a sense our brethren in South India are making this experiment on behalf of the whole body of the Anglican Churches.[11]

Over the next two decades, the horizon darkened further. When, after the disruption of the Second World War, the Church of South India was finally inaugurated in 1947, the encyclical eetter accompanying the documents of the Lambeth Conference from the following year was able to record that "for the first time since the great division of Christendom at the Reformation, an act of union has taken place in which episcopal and non-episcopal traditions have been united."

10 *The Lambeth Conference 1930: Encyclical Letter from the Bishops with Resolutions and Reports* (London: SPCK, 1930), "Encyclical Letter," 26. A substantial section of the report on "The Unity of the Church" was devoted to "The South India Scheme" (123-30).

11 *Ibid.*, 26-27. The term "experiment" in relation to South India recurs in Resolution 40 (51).

The Archbishop of Canterbury also sounded a note of caution, however, and indeed of overt concern: "The Conference gives thanks to God for the measure of unity thus locally achieved. At the same time it records that some features of the Constitution of the Church of South India give rise to uncertainty or grave misgivings in the minds of many."[12] The "serious misgivings" of 1930 had turned "grave," and the Archbishop could no longer so confidently affirm that they ought to be "outweighed by hope."

In fact, the Church of South India became the focus for intense controversy within the Anglican Communion during the central decades of the 20th century. Seeking unity with other churches had increased tensions within the Anglican Communion to a striking degree. In the Church of England, everyone listed in *Crockford's Clerical Directory* was sent a letter asking them to reject the decision of the Convocation allowing partial intercommunion with members of the Church of South India. They were also asked to put up a public notice announcing that members of the Church of South India were not welcome to receive communion in their church, should they happen to be

---

12 *The Lambeth Conference 1948: The Encyclical Letter from the Bishops; Together with Resolutions and Reports* (London: SPCK, 1948), "Encyclical Letter," I.21. The passage quoted here reflects fuller discussion in the report on "The Unity of the Church," which speaks of "many of us" being "exercised, in the later stages of negotiations, by grave and deepening anxiety" (II.42-44).

attending.[13] CMS put out pamphlets in defence of the new church,[14] while in 1947 SPG immediately cancelled its very substantial funding for work in India with only a year's notice. T. S. Eliot called it "the greatest crisis in the Church of England since the Reformation."[15] By the 1970s, the storm had subsided, and the Church of South India took its place alongside the Church of North India, the Church of Pakistan, and the Church of Bangladesh as united churches that are fully part of the Anglican Communion.[16]

Reactions across the Anglican Communion to the formation of the Church of South India in the mid-20th century reveal some of the tensions that were already present at the Lambeth Conference in 1920. If the controversy has more or less died away today, the tensions have continued to cast a shadow over responses to the call of

---

13   Michael Walsh, *Look to the Rock: The Anglican Papalist Quest and the Catholic League* (Norwich: Canterbury Press, 2019), 69. Cf. Lesslie Newbigin's account of his visit to England in 1946, just before being ordained as one of the first bishops for the Church of South India, in *Unfinished Agenda: An Autobiography* (London: SPCK, 1985), 86-90.

14   E.g., Anthony Tyrrell Hanson, *Should an Anglican Support the Church of South India?: Seven Objections Considered* (London: Church Missionary Society, 1953).

15   Sundkler, *Church of South India*, 330.

16   Resolution 14.1 of the 1978 Lambeth Conference was critical here, asking the Archbishop of Canterbury, "in consultation with the Primates, to convene a meeting of Anglican bishops with bishops of Churches in which Anglicans have united with other Christians, and bishops from those Churches which are in full communion with Anglican Churches; and to discuss with them how bishops from these Churches could best play their part in future Lambeth Conferences": *The Report of the Lambeth Conference 1978* (London: CIO Publishing, 1978), 42.

the Appeal to strive for the visible unity of Christ's Church here on earth. Indeed, the events surrounding the founding of the Church of South India must be reckoned at least partially responsible for the inertia that has halted Anglican participation in the formation of united churches since the 1970s. The remainder of this chapter will focus on three of them: the tension between local union and universal communion; the tension between recognition of other churches and commitment to the historic episcopate; and the tension between generous catholicity and Anglican identity.

LOCAL UNION AND UNIVERSAL COMMUNION

The ecumenical ecclesiology of the Lambeth Appeal might be summarised in the following terms: We are called in our time to make visible in and for the sake of mission the unity of the Church that is God's gift, through working for the union of churches in each place and the communion of churches in every place, for which the universal acceptance of the historic episcopate will be essential. Within this framework, the relationship between the union of churches in each place and the communion of churches in every place is crucial. Both are necessary for visible unity.

What had already become apparent by the 1930 Lambeth Conference, however, was that it could be difficult to keep the two in alignment, as moves towards union in South India appeared to threaten the communion of the church that it was hoped would emerge there with continuing Anglican churches. Although it would be "a distinct Province of the Universal Church," the report on "The Unity of the Church" notes that the envisaged united church would not be a member of the Anglican Communion, though still affirming that its formation "will not deprive any members of the united Church, whether Bishops, Clergy or Laity, of any privilege of communion which they have hitherto enjoyed with the Church of England and with the Churches in communion with it."[17] Amongst other emerging concerns, the report commented on the anomaly of a church being in some limited form of communion with the Anglican Communion, and at the same time in communion "with other bodies not in communion with the Anglican Communion."[18] While the report's authors might have appealed at this point to the principle of "economy" as developed in Orthodox tradition, those who endorsed the words quoted above from a 1915 SPG pamphlet might feel that their position had been vindicated: "Union between the Anglican Church and the great Protestant denominations... splits the church into fragments and puts off the day of real union." Whatever one's views, the potential tension between seeking local union and maintaining trans-local communion was becoming evident. By 1948, the report on unity would warn rather sternly that "there are some who are so moved by the urgent need for union in their own areas that they would press towards it, even though the consequence might be the temporary loss of the full communion which they have hitherto enjoyed with other Anglicans."[19]

---

17 *Lambeth Conference 1930*, report on "The Unity of the Church," 125. Cf. "Encyclical Letter," 27, and Resolution 40 (51).

18 *Ibid.*, 128.

19 *Lambeth Conference 1948*, "Report on the Unity of the Church," II.51.

The pain felt at the loss to the Anglican Communion of its church in South India is palpable in the 1948 Lambeth Conference. Two responses to the situation are evident that would be sustained for the next thirty years. The first was that this diminishment of communion between churches in different places for the sake of the union of the churches in one place should never be repeated. As the Archbishop of Canterbury summarised relevant resolutions in his encyclical letter: "we recommend that, in further schemes for reunion, care should be taken to see that they do not, unless for a brief time, put any member of our family of Churches out of communion with it."[20] Ten years later, the encyclical letter for 1958 was able to record hopes for new united churches in Sri Lanka (then called Ceylon), North India and Pakistan that would be from the outset in full communion with the churches of the Anglican Communion. The conference resolutions of 1958 urged that this example be followed by those seeking unity in West Africa, rather than the older model of the Church of South India.[21]

The second response can be seen in the recommendation of Resolution 74 from the 1948 Lambeth Conference, on "A Larger Episcopal Unity," that "bishops of the Anglican Communion and bishops of other Churches which are, or may be, in communion with them should meet together from time to time as an episcopal conference, advisory in character, for brotherly counsel and

---

20 *Lambeth Conference 1948*, I.23. Cf. Res. 56 (d), I.40.

21 *The Lambeth Conference 1958: The Encyclical Letter from the Bishops Together with the Resolutions and Reports* (London: SPCK, 1958), "Encyclical Letter," 1.24. Cf. Resolutions 31-34 (1.38).

encouragement."[22] The report on unity specifically mentions united churches such as the Church of South India in connection with this—though only after identifying the Old Catholics, episcopal Lutherans, and the Orthodox as potential partners.[23] Nonetheless, the resolution expresses an intention to embrace united episcopal churches that included former members of the Anglican church within what subsequent Lambeth Conferences came to refer to as "Wider Episcopal Fellowship." The report's authors envisaged the Anglican Communion exercising a historic role in the cause of Christian unity through this initiative:

> We believe that it is designed in God's providence to gather around itself a number of Churches willing and able to be in communion with one another, but each preserving some points of difference from others, which those others will accept as not hindering their communion with it. In this number we hope that those Churches, which are now endeavouring to recombine the Catholic with the Protestant traditions, will be included when they have grown together and stabilized their Church life.[24]

In fact, the grand plans for such a regular gathering of bishops never materialized. The 1958 Lambeth Conference reaffirmed Resolution 74 from its predecessor, but ten years later the relevant report had to acknowledge that the conference eventually held in

---

22 *Lambeth Conference 1948*, Resolution 74, I.45.

23 *Lambeth Conference 1948*, "Report on the Unity of the Church," II.79.

24 *Ibid.*, II.78.

1964 had involved only thirty-nine bishops, and it recommended for the future a combination of "General" and "Regional" "Episcopal Consultations."[25] By 1978, the focus had shifted entirely to how bishops from united churches in which Anglican churches had been participants and churches in full communion with Anglican churches more generally could participate in future Lambeth Conferences.[26] After that, bishops of the Church of South India have been routinely invited to the Lambeth Conference, along with bishops from the Church of North India, the Church of Pakistan, and the Church of Bangladesh, all established in the early 1970s.

RECOGNITION OF NON-EPISCOPAL CHURCHES AND COMMITMENT TO THE HISTORIC EPISCOPATE

Defusing the tension between union and communion in relation to the united churches of South Asia came at a certain cost. The Lambeth Appeal, in line with the 1919 proposals for church union in South India, hinged on two critical ecclesiological affirmations: ecclesial recognition of non-episcopal as well episcopal churches, as truly churches; and the historic episcopate as necessary for visible

---

25 *Lambeth Conference 1958*, "Encyclical Letter," I.27, and Resolution 16, II.24-25; *The Lambeth Conference 1968: Resolutions and Reports* (London: SPCK, 1968), report on "Renewal in Unity," 147-48.

26 *The Report of the Lambeth Conference 1978* (London: CIO, 1978), Resolution 14 (42).

unity—encompassing the union of churches in each place and the communion of churches in every place. For critics of Anglican ecumenism, there is not so much a tension here as a barely concealed contradiction: how can the historic episcopate be necessary for the Church's unity when it is not necessary for the Church's being as such, which is, according to the creed, one, holy, catholic, and apostolic?[27]

Anglicanism brought into its ecumenical endeavours in the 20th century theological disagreements about episcopacy that went back to the 16th.[28] To some extent, the tension within Anglican ecumenism between ecclesial recognition of non-episcopal churches and commitment to the historic episcopate both transmits and restrains those disagreements. The formation of a united church in South India, however, highlighted two specific difficulties in sustaining that tension when non-episcopal churches responded in earnest to the invitation that had been made in the Lambeth Appeal.

The first difficulty is well-known and indeed is already evident in Section VIII of the Lambeth Appeal itself, not incidentally the longest of the nine. When an Anglican church unites with a non-episcopal church to form a church ordered in the historic episcopate, what

27 Cf. Ingolf Dalferth, "Ministry and Office of Bishop according to Meissen and Porvoo: Protestant Remarks about Several Unclarified Questions" in *Visible Unity and the Ministry of Oversight: The Second Theological Conference Held under the Meissen Agreement between the Church of England and the Evangelical Church in Germany* (London: Church House Publishing, 1997), 9-48.

28 Norman Sykes, *Old Priest and New Presbyter: The Anglican Attitude to Episcopacy, Presbyterianism and Papacy since the Reformation* (Cambridge: Cambridge University Press, 1956).

happens to the existing ministers from that church? The proposal for addressing this question in the Lambeth Appeal drew on the idea of a "Service of Commission" that had already found expression in the 1919 Tranquebar Manifesto.[29] Its articulation, however, was now marked by a fundamental asymmetry: Anglican ministers in these circumstances might receive a "commission" from the non-episcopal church or churches, while the ministers from any non-episcopal church would receive a "commission through episcopal ordination."

Understandably, such a proposal was never likely to commend itself to non-episcopal church partners as a truly mutual action. Moreover, the idea that episcopal ordination, however qualified, is necessary for existing ministers of churches without the historic episcopate for the sake of unity with Anglican churches has been consistently rejected by non-episcopal churches from the 1920s onwards. The report on unity to the 1930 Lambeth Conference noted the impasse that had been reached on this point in conversations between the Church of England and the Church of Scotland and the English Free Churches. The "chief difficulty" had not been about "the basic principles of the united Church," with the vision of the Lambeth Appeal commending itself to all. Rather, the problem was "the interim period which would elapse before all ministers are episcopally ordained," with the Lambeth Appeal's version of "mutual commission" being "found unacceptable by the Free Church representatives."[30]

29 Sundkler, *Church of South India*, 103.

30 *Lambeth Conference 1930*, report on "The Unity of the Church," 118. Cf. the comments of David M. Thompson, "The Unity of the Church in Twentieth-Century England: Pleasing Dream or Common Calling?" in

The alternative approach that eventually emerged in South India was to allow an interim period of anomaly, during which ministers ordained in non-episcopal churches prior to the union would continue to minister in the new united and episcopally ordered church (with certain caveats); by the end of that period, all ministers would be episcopally ordained. While this had been vital to overcoming seemingly intractable differences between the Anglicans and the non-episcopal churches seeking union in South India, it was seen as a major weakness by many other Anglicans elsewhere in the world; indeed, this may have been the critical factor in the estrangement between the new united church and the Anglican Communion reviewed in the previous section. As the report to the 1948 Lambeth Conference summarised the situation, "the establishment of full communion in a complete and technical sense between the Church and the Churches of the Anglican Communion must wait till the ministry of the Church of South India has become fully unified on an episcopal basis," that is, until every individual minister has been episcopally ordained.[31]

The intense criticism the "period of anomaly" attracted from some Anglo-Catholics suggested that their recognition of non-episcopal churches was in fact somewhat limited. In 1941, the official publication of the Catholic League in England denounced the "Plot for a False Union" in South India on the grounds that since those who had not been ordained by a bishop in the historic episcopate could not be recognised as priests, it would result in lay people being given

Unity and Diversity in the Church, ed. R. N. Swanson, Studies in Church History, vol. 32 (Oxford: Blackwell, 1992), 521-23.

31 _Lambeth Conference 1948_, "Report on the Unity of the Church," II.46.

"the right and duty of celebrating Communion" alongside duly ordained ministers.[32] For them, without the historic episcopate, one could not be confident of the validity of ordinations, hence of the efficacy of the sacrament of Holy Communion.

Subsequent attempts across the Anglican Communion to seek local unions with churches not ordered in the historic episcopate could not help but focus on the struggle to square the circle here. A union between churches only makes sense where there is genuine mutual recognition of one another as churches; yet a refusal to accept the ministers of another church unless they are ordained in accordance with the practice of one's own church is bound to be interpreted as the withholding or at least qualification of such recognition. The preferred solution that emerged in the decades after World War II—of a rite of unification of ministries that is not formally an ordination service, but that Anglicans who would like it to be can interpret as such—was integral to the immediate acceptance of the other united churches of South Asia within the Anglican Communion in the early 1970s. It also, however, emerged in the same period as a crucial weakness in the failed scheme for unity between the Church of England and the Methodist Church in Britain, not least as the question of whether such a service did or did not constitute episcopal ordination had to be settled for the purposes of ecclesiastical law.[33] Looking back over

---

32 Walsh, *Look to the Rock*, 60.

33 See, e.g., Colin Buchanan, Eric Mascall, James Packer, and Graham Leonard, *Growing into Union: Proposals for Forming a United Church* (London: SPCK, 1970), 201-2, and W. S. Wigglesworth, "Memorandum" in *Anglican–Methodist Unity: Report of the Joint Working Group 1971* (London: CIO, 1971), 30-31. The report on "Church Unity and the

a lifetime's involvement in the ecumenical movement, including his ministry in South India before and after the union, Lesslie Newbigin identified the determination of the 1948 Lambeth Conference to pursue this route as

> one of those fateful turning-points in human affairs, for if the Lambeth Conference of 1948 had been able to give a cordial welcome to what had been done in South India, I am sure that the whole worldwide movement for unity among the Churches would have gone forward. The Anglican Communion would have fulfilled its true ecumenical vocation to provide a centre around which reformed Christendom can be brought together in unity and in continuity with the historic ministry of the universal Church. That opportunity was lost, and it is not likely to come again.[34]

The second difficulty that came to the fore at the 1948 Lambeth Conference was the understanding of the historic episcopate itself. Already prior to 1920, the formulation had become commonplace that what was required for union with non-episcopal churches was

Church Universal" for the 1958 Lambeth Conference had tried to tread a careful path on this point in its commentary on the proposed service of unification that would inaugurate the new united Churches of North India, Pakistan and Ceylon: "From the Anglican point of view, therefore, the rite is intended to convey everything of value in the Anglican ministry, including the tradition of episcopal ordination" (*Lambeth Conference 1958*, 2.32). Still, to say that someone should be treated *as* episcopally ordained while maintaining they have *not* been episcopally ordained is bound to sound curious.

34 Newbigin, *Unfinished Agenda*, 114.

agreement on "the fact, not the theory" of the historic episcopate.[35]
While properly acknowledging the different theological evaluations
of episcopacy within Anglicanism, the danger of this formula was that
it could appear to empty the historic episcopate of any determinate
meaning at all. The report on unity to the 1930 Lambeth Conference
had tried to address this by identifying five "generally recognised
functions" of the episcopate evident already in the 2nd century and
featuring consistently thereafter:

> When, therefore, we say that we must insist on the Historic
> Episcopate but not upon any theory or interpretation of it, we are
> not to be understood as insisting on the office apart from the func-
> tions. What we uphold is the Episcopate, maintained in successive
> generations by continuity of succession and consecration, as it has
> been throughout the history of the Church from the earliest times,
> and discharging those functions which from the earliest times it
> has discharged.[36]

The parallel report in 1948 built on this point, summarising its
discussion of the episcopate by reaffirming that "room must be left
for varying interpretations of the fact of episcopacy, provided that the
historic succession is maintained, and that the functions of the episcopate are such as have been traditionally assigned to it."[37]

35   Bell ed., *Documents 1916-1920*, 13, 26, 46 *et passim*.

36   *Lambeth Conference 1930*, report on "The Unity of the Church," 115-16.

37   *Lambeth Conference 1948*, "Report on the Unity of the Church," II.50.

Yet the practice of episcopacy in a united church, such as the Church of South India, was bound to be different in some significant ways from that in an Anglican church, with a polity intended to reflect the inheritance of all the uniting churches. How could Anglicans discern whether this new form of episcopacy really corresponded to what was meant by the "historic episcopate"? A year after the founding of the new church, the Lambeth Conference had to record that " a substantial minority" of bishops present were not convinced about the "precise status... in the Church of Christ" of bishops, priests, and deacons ordained in the Church of South India, implicitly because of doubts as to whether all bishops now active within it were truly part of the historic episcopate, despite their having all been ordained by those the Anglican Communion recognized as belonging within it.[38] Not long afterwards, the author of a pamphlet defending the Church of South India to members of the Church of England felt obliged to address the objection that "The Church of South India possesses no real Bishops or Priests."[39] Clearly motivating some of the "uncertainty or grave misgivings in the minds of many" referred to in the 1948 encyclical letter, the question of what content should be given to the famous phrase from the Chicago-Lambeth Quadrilateral, the "historic episcopate" (conspicuously avoided in the Lambeth Appeal itself), remains a continuing challenge for Anglicanism.

---

38 *Lambeth Conference 1948*, Resolution 54 (e), I.39. Cf. "Report on the Unity of the Church," II.47-48.

39 Hanson, *Church of South India*, 1.

GENEROUS CATHOLICITY AND ANGLICAN IDENTITY

In perhaps its most frequently quoted paragraph, the Lambeth Appeal, having identified as its goal "a reunited Catholic Church," paints an inspiring picture of what this might mean:

> The vision which rises before us is that of a Church, genuinely Catholic, loyal to all truth, and gathering into its fellowship all "who profess and call themselves Christians," within whose visible unity all the treasures of faith and order, bequeathed as a heritage by the past to the present, shall be possessed in common, and made serviceable to the whole Body of Christ. Within this unity Christian Communions now separated from one another would retain much that has long been distinctive in their methods of worship and service. It is through a rich diversity of life and devotion that the unity of the whole fellowship will be fulfilled. (Appeal, §IV)

"Christian Communions," including the Anglican Communion, have a "distinctive" contribution to make to the "rich diversity of life and devotion" in a united Catholic Church, the text tells us. Anglicans have always claimed to be part of the Catholic Church, not the whole, and not the centre either, but one part alongside and in relation with others. It is therefore to be expected that as the parts draw closer together in unity, Anglicans would have enduring gifts to bring. In the "vision" sketched out here, however, there would be no Anglican church as such, and presumably in due course of time no Christian who would identify as Anglican, any more than there would be Methodist, Baptist, Orthodox, or Roman Catholic churches and Christians.

The next two Lambeth Conferences upheld this vision while also registering some degree of qualification. The 1930 report on the Anglican Communion has a parallel passage to the one cited above that spells out the implications with greater clarity:

> Our ideal is nothing less than the Catholic Church in its entirety. Viewed in its widest relations, the Anglican Communion is seen as in some sense an incident in the history of the Church Universal. It has arisen out of the situation caused by the divisions of Christendom. It has indeed been blessed of God, as we thankfully acknowledge; but in its present form we believe that it is transitional, and we forecast the day when the racial and historical connections which at present characterise it will be transcended, and the life of our Communion will be merged in a larger fellowship in the Catholic Church.[40]

The 1930 report on unity, however, expresses a note of reservation, as it draws attention to the value of "spiritual resources and... treasures" that have grown "during the period of division" and "must be conserved in the re-united Church."[41] The proposals for union in South India discussed at length elsewhere in the report were clearly part of the background here, with the text acknowledging in a later section the aspiration that the new, united church there "shall give

---

40 *Lambeth Conference 1930*, report on "The Anglican Communion," 153.

41 *Lambeth Conference 1930*, report on "The Unity of the Church," 112.

the Indian expression of the spirit, the thought, and the life of the Church Universal."[42] In order to do this, the church would need to transcend "the racial and historical connections which at present characterise" the Anglican Communion, yet somehow without losing the gifts it has nurtured.

The same tension is discernible at the next Lambeth Conference of 1948. The encyclical letter first vividly reprises the "vision" of 1920 and the "ideal" of 1930: "There would be, in every country where there now exist the Anglican Church and others separated from it, a united Church, Catholic and Evangelical, but no longer in the limiting sense of the word Anglican. The Anglican Church would be merged in a much larger Communion of National or Regional Churches."[43] It then, however, sounds a warning note: "If we were slow to advance the larger cause, it would be a betrayal of what we believe to be our special calling. It would be equally a betrayal of our trust before God if the Anglican Communion were to allow itself to be dispersed before its particular work was done."[44]

Had the Church of South India fulfilled the hope that where there had existed "the Anglican Church and others separated from it," there would be instead "a united Church, Catholic and Evangelical, but no longer in the limiting sense of the word Anglican"? The Anglican Communion had been clear enough that the Church of South India was not an Anglican church, yet its claim to catholicity came under immediate and sustained attack. Was not remaining Anglican a

---

42   *Ibid.,* 126.

43   *Lambeth Conference 1948,* "Encyclical Letter," I.22.

44   *Ibid.,* I.23.

securer way to be catholic than to embark on such risky ecclesial ventures? United churches have continued to have their own challenges around the maintenance of confessional identities, while no Lambeth Conference after 1948 would make a comparable statement on the "transitional" purpose of the Anglican Communion within the providential history of the Catholic Church.

ENDURING TENSIONS?

The three tensions described here—between local union and universal communion, between ecclesial recognition of non-episcopal churches and commitment to the historic episcopate, and between generous catholicity and Anglican identity—are all to some degree intrinsic to Anglican participation in the cause of Christian unity from the late 19th century onwards. One mark of the achievement of the Lambeth Appeal is the extent to which it treated these tensions as balances that could be harmonised in both theology and practical action—as polarities that ultimately point in the same direction, and not zero-sum situations where more of one term must mean less of the other. That confidence was severely tested in the decades that followed, most notably in the Anglican Communion's responses to the formation of the Church of South India. It may be fair to say it began to dissipate completely from the 1970s onwards, as witnessed by the drying-up of Anglican participation in local unions of churches, together with a re-focusing of institutional energy on relations of communion that do not imply the organic transformations of union. "Communion," rather than union, need not mean any change at all for churches that prefer to carry on as before, leaving Anglican and other denominational identities untouched.

Again, these tensions have deeper roots that extend back in Anglican history beyond the 19th century. With regard to the first, between local union and universal communion, the Church of England in the 16th century broke away from the instruments of communion, as it were, that had bound *Ecclesia Anglicana* to Western Catholicism. If reformation rather than union was the justification for that, it was still for the sake of faithfulness to the purposes of Christ for the Church, expressing a conviction that there are moments in history when such faithfulness must be allowed to put in jeopardy existing relationships of universal communion on the part of the local church seeking to be united in the gospel. At the same time, it would be wholly misleading to represent the Church of England as content to exist in isolation from other churches until the beginnings of the modern ecumenical movement in the later 19th century. Regular communication and exchange of people, texts, and ideas with Continental Protestant churches continued through the long English Reformation of the 16th and 17th centuries. Partnership in increasing missionary activity outside Europe, together with the shared experience of the Evangelical Revival across national and confessional boundaries, opened up new horizons in those relationships in the 18th and 19th centuries. From an early stage, the Anglo-Catholic movement brought fresh hope and energy for overcoming the separation between Anglican churches and both the Roman Catholic and the Orthodox communions of churches.[45] Anglican churches understand themselves as part only of the whole church of God, and therefore in a real communion with the whole that requires our attention both because it is a reality to be valued and because it should be visible in common witness to the world.

The second tension identified in this chapter, between ecclesial recognition of non-episcopal churches and commitment to the historic episcopate, has still more obvious origins in the Church of England's participation in the European Reformation. While some Lutheran churches also retained the office of bishop, one of the features that distinguished the Church of England from other reformed churches in the 16th and 17th centuries was its upholding of the threefold order of ministry of deacons, priests, and bishops—together with significant internal debate about the history and significance of these orders. The post-Restoration Church of England affirmed in the Preface to its Ordinal the claim "that from the Apostles' time there have been these Orders of Ministers in Christ's Church; Bishops, Priests, and Deacons," but that did not answer the question of how to evaluate those churches that had emerged from the upheavals of the Reformation on the Continent without those Orders intact, and specifically without bishops. The firm consensus, however, remained that they were indeed churches and should be recognised as such, with Anglican church order nonetheless putting clear limits on how that recognition could be expressed with regard to ordained ministry

---

45 Mark Chapman, *The Fantasy of Reunion: Anglicans, Catholics, and Ecumenism, 1833-1882* (Oxford: Oxford University Press, 2014).

specifically.[46] While Protestant cooperation in missionary endeavour put strains on this position from one side, Anglo-Catholicism challenged it from another, providing space for the expression of the view that without the apostolic ministry of bishops, the apostolicity of the church must necessarily be diminished. In this case, Anglicans would not be able to recognize non-episcopal churches as churches of the same kind and fullness as their own.

There are further historic parallels with regard to the third tension between generous catholicity and Anglican identity—and, indeed, the roots of these three tensions in Anglican history are entangled with one another. The question of the extent to which the Church of England became a "confessional" church in the 16th and 17th centuries is disputed, in part because of the different self-understandings that emerge during that period.[47] Is the Church of England simply the united national church that brings together all faithful English Christians in one body, excluding only those (such as Roman Catholics) who cannot be faithful subjects of the Crown? Does it stand solely on loyalty to the common heritage of the primitive Church, now restored to clearer sight through the labours of Renaissance scholarship and Reformation doctrine, with no claim to any distinctive teaching or practice of its own? (In this case, would it also follow that the Church of England maintain an open stance to deeper unity with other churches prepared

---

46 Sykes, *Old Priest and New Presbyter: The Anglican Attitude to Episcopacy, Presbyterianism and Papacy since the Reformation*, 118-76.

47 See, e.g., Jean-Louis Quantin, *The Church of England and Christian Antiquity: The Construction of a Confessional Identity in the 17th Century* (Oxford: Oxford University Press, 2009).

to share the same stance?[48]) Or, thirdly, is the Church of England an unusual but wholly recognizable member of the family of European reformed churches, imposing a uniformity of worship, order, and doctrine, the peculiar amalgam of which identifies it as different from other members of that family while still uniting it with them against the common enemy of Roman Catholicism? As with the other two tensions, while the questions may become less intense in the 18th century, they by no means disappear. Reframed in the 19th century in significant ways, the three positions just outlined correspond roughly to the three emerging "parties" of the Victorian Church of England: Broad Church, Anglo-Catholic, and Evangelical.

Loss of confidence in Anglicanism's ability to hold these tensions creatively not only undermines its contribution to the cause of Christian unity, but also threatens continuity with its own traditions. The connection between these two underlines the inseparability of Anglican identity from its vocation to seek the unity of Christ's Church. That is why Anglican participation in serious ecumenical endeavour, such as the formation of the Church of South India, is always likely to increase internal tensions about Anglican self-understanding. The challenge is to recognise such participation as a providential opportunity to revisit the tensions, such that reconciliation with other churches can become the occasion for deeper reconciliation within Anglicanism itself and vice-versa. To do so, there has to be confidence that the tensions themselves can be rendered as dynamic and ultimately convergent polarities for a Communion that recognizes itself

---

48   See Yves Congar, *Diversity and Communion*, trans. John Bowden (London: SCM, 1984), 107-25.

as "transitional" in "the history of the Church Universal," to invoke again the language of the 1930 Lambeth Conference. So conceived, the tensions need not play out as contests that are bound to create winners and losers, nor as a dialectic within which Anglicans are sentenced endlessly to circulate.

Nonetheless, it might be recognised in hindsight that there was a price to be paid for the remarkable consensus around Anglican commitment to the unity of the Church that the 1920 Appeal represented. Lang may have been right to discern the work of the Holy Spirit in uniting the bishops in support for the text, but a franker acknowledgement that ecclesiological disagreements within Anglicanism were bound to come to the fore in seeking to realise its compelling vision may have helped to shape more realistic expectations on all sides. Clearer insight that pursuing what the Appeal called the "adventure" of Christian unity would require Anglicans to face some hard theological questions about their own self-understanding—and that this is necessary and productive work within the providence of God—might also have helped to avoid the distancing on the part of many from the Church of South India and other ecumenical initiatives over the century that followed. Properly acknowledged today, we may still hope that, contrary to Newbigin's bleak assessment, the Anglican Communion can find new opportunities to fulfil its true ecumenical vocation, the contours of which emerged so clearly a hundred years ago.[49]

---

49   See further Jeremy Worthen, "The Centenary of the 'Appeal to All Christian People' and the Ecumenical Vocation of Anglicanism," *Theology*, 123/2 (2020): 104-122.

FOUR

The Lambeth Appeal at 100: An Assessment

Michael Root

In the Preface to his *Philosophy of Right*, Hegel famously said that "the owl of Minerva only takes flight at dusk."[1] While the great German philosopher is often infamously obscure, in this case what he metaphorically proposes is clear: we can begin to understand historical realities and processes (i.e., the owl of Minerva takes flight) only when the processes are coming to an end (i.e., at dusk). The retrospective view allows us to see things hidden to the contemporary—although the opposite can also be, in its own way, true. A problem in the application of Hegel's aphorism is that history does not proceed by means of neatly measurable days. We can know when a day is ending, but

---

1   G.W.F. Hegel, *Elements of the Philosophy of Right*, ed. Allen W. Wood, trans. H. B. Nisbet (Cambridge: Cambridge University Press, 1991), 23.

it is hard to know when an historical event or process or movement has reached the sort of terminus that makes retrospect particularly profitable. I have argued elsewhere[2] that we are at the end of at least a certain phase of the history of church unity and division: a phase with roots in the late 19th century, that was truly launched in the years immediately following World War I with the Lambeth Appeal, the Ecumenical Patriarch's Letter to All the Churches, and the organization of the great conferences on Faith and Order and on Life and Work, a phase that expanded and flourished in the decades following World War II.

I believe that over the last few decades we have reached an inflection point. Adapting the language of Thomas Kuhn describing the history of science,[3] I would say that the period of revolutionary ecumenism, when foundational assumptions were called into question and the sphere of the realistically possible seemed to widen, has reached its end and we have entered a time of normal ecumenism, in which concepts, practices, and realities fall into stable patterns resistant to change. The present challenge for ecumenism is how to live within this new situation. What do we do ecumenically when the ecumenical movement stops moving? To meet that challenge, we need a clear sense of the events and processes that got us where we are.

A preliminary side point: every historical analysis is carried out from some perspective. I view Anglican ecumenical engagement from

2 Michael Root, "Normal Ecumenism: Ecumenism for the Long Haul," *Pro Ecclesia* 28/1 (2019): 60–77.

3 Thomas S. Kuhn, *The Structure of Scientific Revolutions*, 4th edn. (Chicago: University of Chicago Press, 2012).

the outside—as a Catholic with a Lutheran background, and as an American. Undoubtedly that perspective helps me see some things not noticed by insiders and blinds me to others.

❈ ❈ ❈

In our contemporary context, a new look at the Lambeth Appeal—and the Anglican ecumenical vocation which the Appeal embodied—makes sense. Reading the Appeal again, I am struck by how much of the conceptuality and strategy of ecumenism throughout the 20th century can already be found there:[4] the foundational appeal to baptism; the centrality of fellowship (we would say *communion*); the stress on visible unity; the combination of an affirmation of diversity with an appeal to offer and receive our various distinctive gifts; the call to self-sacrifice for the sake of unity; the rejection of the absorption of one church by another. Far more than the 1920 Letter of the Ecumenical Patriarch,[5] the Lambeth Appeal outlined the future logic and rhetoric of much of the ecumenical movement.

The Appeal also lays out an Anglican ecumenical strategy that remained relatively consistent through the century. The Appeal was addressed to "all Christian people," unlike the Lambeth Quadrilateral of 1888, which was explicitly concerned with Home Reunion, that is,

---

4   I will cite the Lambeth Appeal and other texts from the 1920 Lambeth Conference from *The Six Lambeth Conferences 1867–1920*, ed. Randall Davidson (London: SPCK, 1929). References to the Appeal will be given parenthetically in the text by section number.

5   See *Documents on Christian Unity, 1920-24*, ed. G. K. A. Bell (Oxford: Oxford University Press, 1924), 44-48.

the unity of Anglicans with Protestants.[6] No distinctions are drawn in the Appeal between different Christian groups. In addition, the Appeal laid out a pragmatic argument for episcopacy, the historic stumbling block for Anglican-Protestant relations, arguing not from necessary conditions of a valid ordination, but from what is most likely to produce a ministry "acknowledged by every part of the Church" (Appeal, §VII). This argument would shape much, but—it will be noted below—not all, Anglican ecumenical discussion of episcopacy in the following decades.

The Appeal, unlike many ecclesiastical texts, is less a statement of a position than the call to a project, to action, to "a new and great endeavor to recover and to manifest to the world the unity of the Body of Christ" (Appeal, §IX), to "an adventure of goodwill and still more of faith" (Appeal, §V). The "principal factors," it says, that have brought about disunity have been "self-will, ambition, and lack of charity" (Appeal, §III). The decisive obstacle to unity is not so much deep doctrinal difference as a kind of moral failure, and it is that moral failure that must be overcome. The Appeal is addressed to the will more than to the intellect.

The natural retrospective question to ask of a project such as this is: Did it succeed? Did it reach its goal? If not, what did it achieve?

Answering that question is strikingly difficult. We obviously are still divided and in that sense the goal has not yet been reached. But what was accomplished? How far did progress extend and along what paths? The problem in responding is not the classical problem of whether the glass is half full or half empty, but whether the glass is almost entirely

---

6 Davidson, *Six Lambeth Conferences*, 122, Res. 11.

empty or close to full. Either answer can be plausibly given.

On the one hand, if the question is the structural relations among the churches, almost nothing has changed. The historic divisions among the strands of the Reformation—Lutheran, Anglican, Presbyterian, and others—are, outside the Indian sub-continent, still in place. The Catholic Church stands where it did one hundred years ago: it does not recognize the orders of Anglican or other "ecclesial communities of the West" and does not sanction eucharistic hospitality or intercommunion with them. Officially, Orthodox relations with the Western churches are where they were in 1920, or perhaps cooler than they were then. If the goal is the *visible unity of the Church*, as that phrase would have been understood at the Lambeth Conference in 1920, then it can seem that little progress has been made.

But on the other hand, in terms of attitudes and practices on the ground, or one might say, in the pew, there have been enormous changes. The barriers in minds and hearts have been significantly dismantled. A 2017 Pew Center study indicated that more than half of both Protestants and Catholics in the United States believe that Catholics and Protestants are more alike than different.[7] A Pew survey of Western Europe found similar results.[8] In the United States, studies of the growing tendency to shift churches during one's lifetime and the rising levels of interchurch marriages also point to changing

7   Pew Research Center, *U.S. Protestants Are Not Defined by Reformation-Era Controversies 500 Years Later* (Washington, DC: Pew Forum on Religion & Public Life, 2017), 22.

8   Pew Research Center, *Five Centuries After Reformation, Catholic-Protestant Divide in Western Europe Has Faded* (Washington, DC: Pew Forum on Religion & Public Life, 2017), 4.

attitudes.[9] Church membership has become much more fluid and differences of church affiliation often count for less. If "God wills fellowship" and *fellowship* is understood as we often understand it colloquially (and not as ecclesial communion), then fellowship across the ecclesial boundaries is far greater today than it was in 1920. Ecclesial division has often become quite friendly, even comfortable. One might think that we have almost entered the ecumenical promised land, if only Catholics and Orthodox would lighten up on intercommunion.

My claims are, of course, sweeping and there is not space here to back them up further. My general point is only that the ecumenical movement—and the Lambeth Appeal as one of the initiating events of the movement—has ended up somewhere it did not intend or foresee. We need to think about this.

In this brief essay, I want to look at three ways the project of the Appeal has run into difficulties. In each case, I can do little more than give a sketch of an analysis and argument. The three challenges relate to the ecumenical goal of full visible unity, to questions of authority and the apostolic deposit, and to episcopacy.

❄ ❄ ❄

First, the Appeal, appropriately enough, does not lay out just what a visibly united Church would look like; that is the task of the ecumenical project to which the Appeal calls. An examination of the

---

9   Pew Research Center, *U.S. Religious Landscape Survey: Religious Affiliation: Diverse and Dynamic* (Washington, DC: Pew Forum on Religion & Public Life, 2008), 22.

preceding Lambeth Conference and the Conferences succeeding, however, makes clear what is presumed: an understanding of what unity entails that would come to be, to a significant degree, embodied in the New Delhi and Nairobi statements on unity from the World Council of Churches.[10] At the local and national levels, the goal was organic unity, which implied in most minds the disappearance of distinct church bodies, the end of so-called parallel jurisdictions. At the international and world levels, the goal was some form of fellowship or communion among essentially autonomous national or regional churches. The international side of this bipartite picture of the ecumenical goal has steadily developed over the last hundred years, with promising explorations of the nature of conciliar fellowship and the need for some sort of primacy. Far more problematic has been the goal of organic unity.

Concrete work in pursuit of organic unity at the local, regional, and national levels has almost entirely been an extension of the project of "Home Reunion," that is, an Anglican and Protestant project. It was pursued in a variety of reunion schemes of Anglican and Protestant churches in different parts of the world—for instance, the East Africa discussions[11] and the Consultation on Church Union in the United States.[12] Decades of effort were expended in elaborating and promoting

10 Günther Gassmann, ed., *Documentary History of Faith and Order 1963–1993*, Faith and Order Paper, no. 159 (Geneva: WCC Publications, 1993), 3.

11 Frieder Ludwig, *Church and State in Tanzania: Aspects of Changing Relationships, 1961–1994* (Leiden: Brill, 1999), 73-74.

12 A comprehensive history of the Consultation on Church Union can be found in Keith Watkins, *The American Church That Might Have Been: A*

these schemes. Outside of South Asia, however, these efforts failed and have been, to my knowledge, almost universally abandoned (and, to a striking degree, forgotten). Beyond the specific issues that proved insoluble, the sober reality had to be faced. For the most part, laity and rank-and-file clergy simply did not want organic unity as it had been imagined.[13] A survey of the reactions of the various denominations involved in the American Consultation on Church Union found unhappiness not only with the plan of union proposed, but "a general unreadiness for any structural pattern" of unity.[14]

The recognition that plans for organic unity were proving widely unacceptable was instrumental in the rise of proposals for *full communion* as an alternative model of the ecumenical goal. Within such full communion, the churches would remain fully autonomous, without any move toward a common structure, while mutually and fully recognizing each other's faith, sacraments, and orders, establishing full eucharistic hospitality, and exchangeability of clergy. The

---

History of the Consultation on Church Union (Eugene, Oregon: Pickwick Publications, 2014).

13 A survey conducted in connection with the 1957 North American Faith and Order Assembly had already found a general lack of interest in organizational merger among Protestant laity and clergy; see Walter G. Muelder, "Institutionalism in Relation to Unity and Diversity" in *The Nature of the Unity We Seek: Official Report of the North American Conference on Faith and Order, September 3–10, 1957, Oberlin, Ohio*, ed. Paul S. Minear (St. Louis: Bethany Press, 1958), 92f., 101.

14 Consultation on Church Union, "The Significance of the Responses to A Plan of Union for the Church of Christ Uniting," *Mid-Stream* 12 (1972): 177.

goal of organic unity came to be replaced by "reconciled diversity."[15] Theorists of "full communion" (among whom, I must admit, I played a minor role) did insist that such full communion agreements must include effective structures of joint decision-making on issues of common concern.[16] In practice, however, such structures, when created, were stripped of any true decision-making capacity.[17] The result has not been something one might honestly call "full communion", but

---

15   For a history of the discussions and actions that produced the shift toward such an understanding of full communion as the ecumenical goal, see Harding Meyer, *That All May Be One: Perceptions and Models of Ecumenicity*, trans. William G. Rusch (Grand Rapids: Eerdmans, 1999).

16   See, for example, Günther Gassmann and Harding Meyer, eds., *The Unity of the Church: Requirements and Structure*, LWF Report, no. 15 (Geneva: Lutheran World Federation, 1983) and Michael Root, "'Reconciled Diversity' and the Visible Unity of the Church" in *Community-Unity-Communion: Essays in Honour of Mary Tanner*, ed. Colin Podmore (London: Church House Publishing, 1998), 237-51.

17   Note the subtle shifts in the description of the activities of a Joint Commission between the original US Episcopal-Lutheran *Concordat of Agreement* (in Lutheran-Episcopal Dialogue—Series III, *"Toward Full Communion" and "Concordat of Agreement"*, ed. William A. Norgren and William G. Rusch [Minneapolis: Augsburg, 1991], para. 10) and the later *Called to Common Mission* (Evangelical Lutheran Church in America, *Called to Common Mission: A Lutheran Proposal for a Revision of the Concordat of Agreement* [Chicago: Evangelical Lutheran Church in America, 1999], para. 23). In the latter, all activities of the commission come under the verb "to facilitate." I was a member of the drafting committee that produced *Called to Common Mission*; the committee resisted the evisceration of joint decision-making, but the change was forced by the churches.

rather "friendly division with porous borders."[18] Too often, instead of following the Lund Principle (that churches should act together in all matters except those in which conviction compel them to act separately), churches in such relations of full communion follow an anti-Lund Principle—they do separately all except what necessity or expedience requires them to do together. As Reinhard Hütter has put it, 'reconciled diversity' has become 'reconciled indifference'.[19]

Anglicanism has been extensively, but not entirely, resistant to this shift in ecumenical understanding, thanks particularly to the work of Dame Mary Tanner.[20] The U.S. Episcopal Church, however, made an important move toward accepting such a new pattern in a Declaration on Unity in 1979.[21] The Anglican Communion and the Church of England proved more resistant, but uncertainty is evident.

---

18 Michael Root, "The Unity of the Church and the Reality of the Denominations," *Modern Theology* 9 (1993): 385–401.

19 Reinhard Hütter, "Catholic Ecumenical Doctrine and Commitment— Irrevocable and Persistent: Unitatis Redintegratio as a Case of an Authentic Development of Doctrine" in *Dogma and Ecumenism: Vatican II and Karl Barth's* Ad Limina Apostolorum, ed. Matthew Levering, Bruce L McCormack, and Thomas Joseph White (Washington, DC: Catholic University of America Press, 2019), 279.

20 Mary Tanner, "The Goal of Unity in Theological Dialogues Involving Anglicans" in *Einheit der Kirche: Neue Entwicklungen und Perspektiven*, ed. Günther Gassmann and Peder Nørgaard-Højen (Frankfurt a.M.: Verlag Otto Lembeck, 1988), 69-78; Mary Tanner, "The Goal of Visible Unity: Yet Again" in *The Unity We Have and the Unity We Seek: Ecumenical Prospects for the Third Millennium*, ed. Jeremy Morris and Nicholas Sagovsky (London: T & T Clark, 2003), 179-90.

21 *Journal of the General Convention of the Protestant Episcopal Church in the United States of America* (New York: The Episcopal Church, 1979), B-40.

The 1988 Lambeth Conference notes a disagreement whether full communion or organic unity is the ecumenical goal. In its descriptions of *full communion*, however, one can see a tendency to replace "common decision-making" with "mutual consultation."[22] The 2008 Kyoto Report of the Inter-Anglican Standing Commission on Ecumenical Relations continues to see such "denominational communion" agreements as stages on the way to true unity,[23] but does that way of seeing things correspond to the way such agreements actually function?

Ecumenism is not primarily about relations among theologies and ideal conceptual constructs of our traditions, but about relations among churches, which are concrete social bodies embedded in history. Churches, especially churches such as the Anglican or Catholic or Lutheran churches, which take in large swathes of the population, are not immune to deep trends in secular life. To what degree have the transformations in our attitudes toward one another been the result of a true change of ecumenical heart and to what degree have they been the result of the penetration of our ecclesial outlook by dispositions typical of consumer capitalism? Has the animosity between church and chapel or even between Anglican and Catholic receded because the differences are seen less like the difference between truth and falsity and more like the difference between Coca-Cola and Pepsi,

22 Lambeth Conference 1988, *The Truth Shall Make You Free: The Lambeth Conference 1988*, The Reports, Resolutions & Pastoral Letters from the Bishops (London: Anglican Consultative Council, 1988), 147, sect. 97; cf. 144, sect. 82.

23 Inter-Anglican Standing Commission on Ecumenical Relations, *The Vision Before Us: The Kyoto Report*, comp. and ed. Sarah Rowland Jones (London: Anglican Communion Office, 2009), 34.

a matter of consumer preference? Is part of the resistance to organic unity akin to the resistance to monopolies that would limit consumer choice? Are full communion agreements that essentially leave the churches just as they are the result of a new-found respect for diversity in communion, or an accommodation to the dynamics of the market? My worry is that the limited full communion agreements—attractive in part because, unlike organic unity, they have proven achievable— will not be waystations on the path to unity, but false substitutes for unity, where ecumenism goes to die. Here the vision of the Lambeth Appeal must be held to.

※ ※ ※

A second challenge to the ecumenical program of the Lambeth Appeal came from the opposite direction. The Appeal was comprehensive, addressed to all Christians, including Catholics and Orthodox. Inevitably, issues raised by the Reformation of the 16th century had to be taken up. Since 1920, however, some classical issues raised by the Reformation, especially on authority and tradition, have been turned on their heads. In the 16th and still in the 19th century, a common Protestant and Anglican complaint about Rome was that it had innovated; it had refused to accept the normativity of the faith once and for all delivered to the saints and added new doctrines, like the immaculate conception of Mary and papal infallibility. A crucial issue for Newman and later between Newman and Pusey in the mid-19th century was the development of doctrine. Newman became Catholic when he had worked out for himself an understanding of the development of doctrine. Pusey in his Eirenicons of the 1860s continued to reject Newman's understanding of development. The consensus of the Fathers is the limit of doctrine. Here the Anglo-Catholic Pusey was a variant realization of a standard Reformation attitude toward a normative apostolic deposit, which binds the Church of later ages.[24]

In recent decades, the tables have turned. In the growing divide between Anglicans (and a significant number of Protestant bodies) on the one hand and Catholics and Orthodox on the other over the meaning and significance of sexuality, both for ordination and for same-sex relations, the traditional positions have reversed. Catholics claim to be bound by an apostolic teaching which they have no authority to change, while Anglicans and others claim a freedom for doctrinal development. The merits of the respective claims are a topic for another time. My concern is the way this development affects an important aspect of the project of the Lambeth Appeal, namely, its comprehensive character.

While I have described the new difference as a reversal of the traditional pattern, for a certain Catholic reading of the Reformation with a long pedigree, the reversal was predictable. Within a year of Luther's posting of his 95 Theses on indulgences, Catholic critics began to contend that an appeal to the sole supremacy of Scripture, that is, to an unchanging deposit of the past, without binding organs of interpretation, would collapse into "private judgment," whether exercised by individuals or groups, since the historical deposit could

---

24   An excellent discussion of the Newman-Pusey exchange can be found in Mark D. Chapman, *The Fantasy of Reunion: Anglicans, Catholics, and Ecumenism, 1833–1882* (Oxford: Oxford University Press, 2014), 68-130.

be hermeneutically twisted at will.[25] In his blunt words at the 2008 Lambeth Conference, Cardinal Walter Kasper, at that time President of the Pontifical Council for the Promotion of Christian Unity, saw the Anglican decisions on the cluster of sexuality questions as moving Anglicanism into a more clearly Protestant orbit.[26]

Such words are naturally irritating to many Anglican sensibilities, but I want to raise the larger background question about the Anglican ecumenical vocation as elaborated in the Lambeth Appeal. The comprehensive character of the Appeal fit with a certain Anglican self-image as a tradition at once Catholic and Protestant. I need not remind Anglicans that just how Anglicanism is both Catholic and Protestant has been a consistently controverted matter. Especially in the present ecumenical situation, careful reflection is needed on just what are the foundations and limits of the Church's decision-making power, an issue at the very center of the Reformation debates. Just what is and is not amendable in the life of the Church, on what basis is such a distinction to be made, and who makes such a distinction by what processes of discernment? Catholics decide on matters Anglicans think not subject to human judgment (the immaculate conception of Mary, for example) and Anglicans decide on matters Catholics think not subject to human judgment (the ordination of women or matters of same-sex ethics). The issues here are not simple. My worry is that the impulses

25 Johannes Tetzel was making such an argument in May 1518; see David V. N. Bagchi, *Luther's Earliest Opponents: Catholic Controversialists, 1518–1525* (Minneapolis: Fortress Press, 1991), 86.

26 Walter Kasper, "Roman Catholic Reflections on the Anglican Communion," *Information Service, Pontifical Council for Promoting Christian Unity* 129 (2008): 148.

of Catholicism and the Reformation, perhaps moving on converging paths in the mid-20th century, may now be moving decisively in different directions. Anglicanism may think of itself as a bridge church, but a bridge is not a secure place to be when the land masses on the two sides of the bridge are moving in opposite directions.

※ ※ ※

A third challenge to the program of the Lambeth Appeal has been more focused. About one-third of the text of the Appeal discusses the more pragmatic strategy on bishops to which I have already referred. Rather than arguing that episcopacy in apostolic succession is somehow the normative, divinely willed polity, the Appeal suggests that episcopacy is the most practical way to achieve an ordained ministry acceptable to the widest number of Christians. Episcopacy and episcopal succession has consistently been the hard nut to crack in Anglican-Protestant relations and the strategy suggested by the Appeal held out promise. Such a strategy has not been easy to pursue; with some frequency Anglican churches have entered into or even initiated ecumenical discussions only to fail to achieve unity among themselves on just what kind of agreement on episcopacy is needed.[27] Even so, a survey of ecumenical discussions shows the general failure of the Lambeth Appeal's strategy on episcopacy. In the case of the US Consultation on Church Union, the reliance from the beginning on an argument for episcopacy along purely pragmatic lines was one of

27 This tendency is noted in David M. Paton, *Anglicans and Unity* (London: A.R. Mowbray, 1962), 50-52.

a number of reasons for the consultation's failure.[28] When Anglicans have reached agreement on episcopacy with Protestant churches, the churches have generally been Lutheran or Methodist, traditions not theologically opposed to episcopacy and including some churches which already had bishops, though often not in episcopal succession

I raise this point to note a limit on the picture of ecumenism as a sharing of gifts, a picture already implicit in the Appeals' talk of churches inappropriately holding on to gifts that should be shared (§II). Insufficient attention has been given to the problem of what I call the dead mouse gift, a gift that may be valuable to the giver but undesired by the recipient, as a cat might present a dead mouse to its owner as a kind of present. (When I was a child, the family cat, Sancho Panza, would on occasion present a dead mouse in this way to my mother, who was definitely not pleased.) Receptive ecumenism and ecumenism as a gift-exchange proposed shifting the focus of ecumenical discussion from arguing over differences, or seeing differences as at least potentially problematic, to seeing differences as something to share.[29] This shift can be helpful. The problem comes when a tradition sees some aspect of its life as a gift to be shared, convinced that others will come to see the virtues of the gift, while others fail to see those virtues, or even see the gift as unacceptable, as incompatible with settled theological convictions.

---

28 Watkins, *American Church*, 142.

29 The most recent statement from the Anglican-Roman Catholic International Commission welcomes the notion of receptive ecumenism; Anglican-Roman Catholic International Commission (ARCIC III), *Walking Together on the Way: Learning to Be the Church—Local, Regional, Universal: Erfurt 2017* (London: SPCK, 2018), para. 16.

The problem of the dead mouse gift can be addressed only by theological argument. Why is this gift desirable or perhaps necessary for a truly common life? The greater the resistance, the more robust the argument needs to be. Questions of polity have been so central to the post-Reformation debates of Anglicans and Protestants that something more than the pragmatic argument of the Lambeth Appeal will be needed. I believe that one factor in the success of the Anglican-Lutheran proposals in Northern Europe (the Porvoo Agreement),[30] Canada (the Waterloo Agreement),[31] and the US was the elaboration of a more-than-pragmatic argument for episcopal succession in the international Anglican-Lutheran Niagara Report of 1987.[32]

The phenomenon of the ecumenical dead mouse gift points to a wider reality. A church's ecumenical outlook may appear in one light from within that church and in another light from outside that church. The Lambeth Quadrilateral is generally seen as a forward-looking and potentially helpful proposal by Anglicans, but it has been seen in other terms by non-Anglicans. Samuel McCrea Cavert, an American Presbyterian who was Executive Secretary of

---

30 *Together in Mission and Ministry. The Porvoo Common Statement with Essays on Church and Ministry in Northern Europe* (London: Church House Publishing, 1993).

31 Joint Working Group of the ACC and the ELCiC, *Called to Full Communion: A Study Resource for Lutheran-Anglican Relations, Including The Waterloo Declaration* (Toronto: Anglican Book Centre, 1998).

32 Anglican-Lutheran International Continuation Committee, *The Niagara Report: Report of the Anglican-Lutheran Consultation on Episcope, Niagara Falls, September 1987* (Cincinnati: Forward Movement Publications, 1988).

the Federal Council of Churches and then its successor the National Council of Churches for almost forty years, viewed the Lambeth Quadrilateral as a very politely phrased invitation for everyone to come together by becoming Anglican.[33]

I would guess that if the fathers of the Lambeth Appeal—Frank Weston, Randall Davidson, George Bell—could return today and see the ecumenical distance still to travel, they would be disappointed. Too many things are as they were. Anglicans often remain too Protestant for many Catholics and too Catholic for many Protestants. Perhaps one cause of the excessive optimism of the authors of the Appeal lay in their diagnosis of the cause of division, which they found in "self-will, ambition, and lack of charity." In my 35 years of ecumenical work, I have encountered a great deal of charity, not that much self-will, and even less ambition (if one takes up ecumenism out of ambition, one is not very smart). And yet, we remain apart. Did the Lambeth bishops underestimate the role of incompatible theological convictions, held in at least minimal good faith, as a decisive factor in our divisions? We can repent of our self-will—or try to: repentance is itself not something called up at will and just what calls for repentance is too often not clear—and still remain divided. Perhaps ill-will suffices for division, but goodwill alone does not suffice for true unity.

※ ※ ※

33　Samuel McCrea Cavert, *The American Churches in the Ecumenical Movement, 1900–1968* (New York: Association Press, 1968), 28.

As I said at the outset, I believe the ecumenical re-configuration of the last 100 years has, at least for the North Atlantic churches, reached a new stability, difficult to disturb. Our ecumenical challenge is not that of Lambeth 1920. We need today to find ways of manifesting and witnessing the unity we have, while frankly admitting the ongoing significance of our disagreements. Unity cannot be forced or willed. Our calling may be to an obedient, but unforgetting, patience. We may have to wait, and wait a long time, for greater unity. That may be the obedience to which we are called, but we must not forget that division contradicts what we know to be true, that we are at a fundamental level one in Christ. Such an obedient and unforgetting patience is, in its own way, an adventure of goodwill and of faith.

PART II

Contemporary Theological Perspectives

❋ ❋ ❋

FIVE

Is There a Rationale for the Anglican Communion?

Ephraim Radner

The purpose of these remarks is to sketch a rationale for the Anglican Communion; *rationale* in the sense of answering the question *why?* Why an Anglican Communion, and why this one or some other? I am going to suggest that we need a thick rationale, not a thin one such as we have been hanging onto, in various guises, over the past few decades. Thin rationales for communion tend to focus on one or two things only—a rule, a precedent, a principle. They tend to rely on divine presumption: since this is what God is already after, we don't need to worry about our role too much. And they tend frankly to end up subtracting, not contributing to communion, because what doesn't fit the rule or what seems to demand too much is easily discarded or ignored. A thick rationale, by contrast, is filled with a range of ends, demands lots of work, imagines God doing all kinds of things. And it results in a wider and deeper communion as a result. The contrast of thin and thick as I use it (people use it in different ways) is ultimately metaphysical, and speaks to the nature of reality, in a manner explained by, among others, the philosopher Robert Nozick. Reality is full, complex, varied, ever challenging, and *must* be described as such. So is communion.

The Anglican Communion, in its historical emergence, was informed by thicker rationales, culminating in the 1920 Lambeth Conference's "Appeal to All Christian People," which dealt with attitudes and actions of all the churches, and finally with the nature of God. Over the past decades, however, we've been holding on to thinner and thinner rationales. For instance, we say that the Anglican Communion is a vehicle for promoting certain forms of social progress; or that the Anglican Communion is a body that articulates and develops certain dogmatic truths of the Gospel; or again, that the Anglican Communion is a place where different people come together in benign respect, according to certain strict principles of governance or limited legal relationships. Precisely because these kinds of rationales are thin, they do not cohere with one another, nor do they offer the means or openings to engaging, including, reforming, and mutually remaking one another. There is, as a result, a fair degree of conflict in our midst—conflicts between thin rationales, you might say—such that the Anglican Communion is today characterized by churches that are *not* in communion with each other, or that are in something called "impaired communion," or that ignore one another, or are practically ignorant of each other, and so on. At the same time, individual members have left the Communion for other churches in search of some better rationale for their commitments. All this is what happens with thin rationales: they cannot bear the weight of actual ecclesial reality, which is thick. A thick rationale has room for the Church as it is, even if it makes heavy demands upon the Church's members.

I certainly make no claims to knowing much about this. But one thing I bring to the discussion is simply having lived *through* changes in rationale, as well as through the conflicts themselves: through thick and thin, or rather *from* thick *to* thin.

My first work of ordained ministry was as a young American Episcopal priest in the Anglican Church of Burundi, working along-side British Church Mission Society (CMS) missionaries. It was a tough row to hoe. American smug self-confidence meets British know-it-all-ness, amid an alien world with its own gifts of faith. I was initially sent for a couple months to CMS's then training college, Crowther Hall, in Birmingham. I could feel myself being sucked into a heavy atmosphere of smiling British evangelical Anglian re-education—getting me to learn to trust my betters, learn the well-ordered ropes, and squeeze out my callow, New World self-assertions. They were right to be anxious about me, as it turned out. In any case, it was with a certain trepidation and resistance that I then joined my British colleagues in Burundi, within a classic mix of mutual cultural suspicions.

What ended up happening, though, was that the British and the American in this case became deep and fiercely loyal friends. It was simple, really: our inculcated and sparring confidences inevitably dissolved, over time, in the face of the tremendous challenges we shared within our lives and work. With the burdens came often hard-won blessings of breaking through a far more difficult set of cultural demands embodied in our common life with Burundi colleagues and neighbors—Anglicans, Catholics, government employees, police, merchants, soldiers, goatherds. Hard-won indeed, though real. There were illnesses, lies, wants, injustices, AIDS, arrests, the memories and ongoing realities of violence, and the search for a Gospel stronger than our wretched incapacities and angers. Not once, but many times, this reality drove us all—British, American, Burundi—literally to our knees. We were driven there by each other, to be sure, but eventually and necessarily *with* each other; and it was clear, at last, *for* each other too.

That is simply an intimation of the "thick" realities I want us to consider. But it also informs my understanding of the great proclamation, "God wills fellowship," a statement that functioned in a real way as a kind of undergirding rationale for the Anglican Communion over several decades. Perhaps it still does. But those words shifted in their implications, over the years, from thick to thin.

❆ ❆ ❆

The phrase itself, "God wills fellowship," comes from the 1920 Lambeth Appeal (Resolution 9). It emerged from and looked into a rich and difficult reality of human life ordered by God in Christ within a fallen world—that is what made it "thick." Then it became almost an ecclesial ideology within mid-20th-century Anglicanism, which began thinning it out. Finally it faded into an anodyne mantra of respectful coexistence or condescending tolerance under the aegis of ill-defined "bonds of affection."[1] If the phrase *God wills fellowship* is to remain a useful one for us, we must examine how it can maintain its thick meaning. To do that, let me distinguish two ways in which we can understand the phrase: providentially and obedientially. Holding the two senses together is what a thick rationale requires.

The term *will*, as in "God wills fellowship," can mean at least two things. The divine will can refer to a divine action: what God wills, God does, by a metaphysical equivalence. "For he spake, and it was [done]; he commanded, and it stood fast" (Ps. 33:9). "The plans of the Lord stand firm forever, the purposes of his heart through all generations" (Ps. 33:11). In this sense, God's will for fellowship means that such fellowship is already at work, already happening, perhaps already in place. This is how some read the next sentence of the Lambeth resolution: "By God's own act this fellowship was made in and through Jesus Christ, and its life is in his Spirit." Fellowship is already "made," and what is left, as the Appeal put it, is to "manifest" that fellowship in a kind of temporal or visible way.[2]

But the divine will can also refer to a kind of command, a divine desire that exists in relation to only *potential* human obedience. In

---

1 See originally *Bonds of Affection: Proceedings of ACC-6* (Badagry/London: Anglican Consultative Council, 1984). Cf. *The Windsor Report* (London: Anglican Communion Office, 2004).

2 According to the fundamental ecclesiological claim of the Encyclical Letter for the 1920 Lambeth Conference, "the one body exists. It needs not to be made, nor to be remade, but to become organic and visible.... We have only to discover it, and to set free its activities." See Randall Davidson, ed., *The Six Lambeth Conferences, 1867–1920* (London: SPCK, 1929), "Lambeth Conference 1920," p. 12.

this sense, God's will for fellowship is something that can be opposed, ignored, frustrated. Over this divine will stands the hovering threats of something like Leviticus 26 or Deuteronomy 28: "if you hearken not to my commands"—if, that is, in the culminating warning of Hebrews, "they escaped not who refused him that spake on earth, much more [shall not] we [escape], if we turn away from him that [speaketh] from heaven." In this sense of the divine will, it is possible to sin *against* communion, and thus, in consequence, actually to "destroy my people" (cf. Isa. 3:12; Hos. 4:6), picking apart the very fellowship that God has offered and commanded.

I point out this difference in the sense of divine *will*—hence, the difference between communion as given and communion as commanded, and thus potentially opposed or destroyed—not because these two senses are mutually contradictory. They are not necessarily. Rather, our own sense of vocation with respect to communion is probably differently grasped depending on how we frame God's willing of fellowship, and this can go in thicker or thinner ways.

Let us look at the first sense of the divine will, that is, that history embodies God's purpose. We could call this the "providential" sense, taken more and more as a sufficient understanding of God's willing of communion. Apart from the obediential aspect, this providentialist understanding has in fact thinned out our communion rationales considerably.

※ ※ ※

The notion of the Anglican Communion as a providential enactment partially trades on this understanding of God's will. That judgment regarding providence is, in my mind, a fair one up to a point: the Anglican Communion emerged only over time; it was not humanly planned. Cranmer certainly didn't imagine it. Probably his own sense of the coherent national church logically stood in tension with where things ended up—a familiar tension today with respect to the relationship of provincial autonomy and communion coherence. Even when theologically and strategically self-conscious British Anglican missionary efforts took off by the late seventeenth century, there was no sense that networks or fellowships of churches, bound to these efforts, would form across the globe. It just happened, so to speak, through a bevy of actions, expenditures, lives, mixed motives, and the rest, which historians have only really begun to sift. The idea that there *was* a "communion," characterized by the qualifier "Anglican," was, as we know, only first articulated clearly in the mid-nineteenth century, at a time when this grab-bag of missionary and colonial labors and effects were retrospectively evaluated as something God was up to all along. Even at this point, the missionary Anglican Communion had little clear theological identity.

Nonetheless, I would argue that this knotted history was, by definition, a thick one, filled with joys and sighs, brokenness and transformation. There was something deep about it. Just reading accounts of mission around the globe over the centuries, and of the struggle of young churches and their laity and leaders to grow in faith and witness, can fill one with emotion, both troubled and joyous. By the early 20th century at the great Anglican missionary gatherings and congresses of the time (e.g., the 1908 Pan-Anglican Congress in London), the notion of God having a fellowship plan, as it were, had been lifted up as a motivating vision: all the "races" of the earth—Chinese, European,

African, Indian, Polynesian, and so on—joining each other, complementing each other, bound to each other in the diverse and literally polychromatic body of Christ, in fulfilment of God's reconciling will.[3] The idea of such a worldwide, international, divinely-ordered fellowship after World War I, when the 1920 Lambeth Conference launched its Appeal, was no longer one of untarnished confidence, to be sure; and after World War II, the idea was fraught with a sometimes overwhelming sense of difficulty. Yet drawing together the peoples of the earth in Christ was also exciting. Books, pamphlets, conferences, strategies, serious deliberations proliferated. People like Max Warren at the CMS, and then Stephen Bayne in the emerging Communion offices, were listened to with an aroused and pointed enthusiasm. I suppose I began my own training and ministry on the coattails of this excitement, which was still residually dispersed into the late 1970s.

The 1920 statement that "God wills fellowship," with the formal Appeal in which the statement was embedded, was thus a further stage in this emerging judgment that had first been voiced in the 19th century. It was now an articulation bound to a moral *demand*, colored by the horrendously sorrowful experiences of World War I and the wreckage left in its wake, in which churches were themselves implicated. This fellowship is what God wills. And the certainty of the belief was founded on a further judgment about the shape of God's actions. For now the Anglican bishops gathered at Lambeth could state that,

---

3 See *Mankind and the Church: Being an Attempt to Estimate the Contribution of Great Races to the Fulness of the Church of God, by Seven Bishops* (London: Longmans, Green and Co., 1907), a volume preparatory to the 1908 Pan-Anglican Congress.

whatever the confusions so clearly evident in human society, the outcomes and energies of Anglican life around the world had manifested something identifiably *expected* theologically, because it was morally, that is divinely, necessary. Lambeth could call for communion or fellowship because, looking about at its members and at the history they embodied, it had *recognized* that the communion somehow and so vulnerably existing amid its own gathering was exactly what God wills. Even if sensing the powerful forces ranged against it, that recognition was a claim about the very nature of history. It had emerged from the smoke and dust, by grace. Whatever communion itself may be, the notion that communion is given by God and then taken in the course of a great divine tide of time remains with us.

But taken on its own, the theory in fact has turned out to be rather thin. There is, first, the problem of human definitions of history's march excluding the slowpokes. If one is on the allegedly right side, the rest who are not on that side inevitably can be brushed aside as beside the point. When driven by human dynamics, the "right side of history" makes fellowship itself contract into smaller and smaller networks of members. Too much human confidence in providence leads to too little communion. The great claims of the 1920 Appeal and its accompanying formal Letter envisaged the vastness of "Mankind," as they put it, as its object: the range of Christendom and all its churches and traditions, their long struggles and hopes, the breadth of the globe. It was this breadth that was seen as God's will, the truth of God filling the earth, "as the waters cover the sea" (Hab. 2:14).

Just such claims make little sense in today's littered and embattled landscape, Anglicanism itself being a contrastive exemplar. We now live in human history's greatest movement of peoples across the globe—well over 250 million migrants and refugees, who are both the result and cause of profound political conflict. The Christian faith continues to grow in the midst of this turmoil in places like Africa and Asia (and for the first time in centuries in North Africa as well), and among immigrants within the West. Yet Western Anglican churches are both contracting numerically at an astonishing rate and continuing to recoil at the very faith arising from international reordering and effervescence, as if *this* kind of messy providence is unassimilable.

A second, rather practical problem with the singularly providentialist view of God's will for our Communion is that others seem to be riding history's putative currents far more successfully than our various Anglican vessels have managed to do. The local and international legal cultures of the world have proven more powerful, adept, and efficient at the progressivist vision. Among confessionalists, Roman Catholics are clearly way ahead, while evangelical and reformed parachurch organizations, with their well-tuned congregational outcomes, do far better than Anglicans in most places. In all cases, the right side of history seems centered, according to these thinned out providentialist rationales, *outside* of most Anglican ecclesial circles altogether.

Logically, of course, providence cannot be a rationale for anything, including for our Communion. One has to know not only the end of the story but how one gets from one part of the story to the other in order to claim that what has happened can tell us anything about why we are doing something for the future. I just got back from a short trip to Tunisia. Wandering through the weed-infested, garbage strewn, mosque- and condominium-shadowed ruins of Carthage and the ancient pathways of Perpetua, Cyprian, and Augustine is a sobering experience. At the time, the rationale for their ecclesial vocations would have been hard to fathom on the basis of some providential history of ecclesial integrity over the decades. One is always forced to look outside one's own location to understand providence itself—a warning to both Western and non-Western Anglicans who are confident in their historical rectitude.

God may well will fellowship in a sense that demands our full confidence in that divine will's final accomplishment. God gets what God wants, thus God will *get* fellowship. But we should not assume that you and I will be there when he gets it. Certainly not based on where we now stand. The end must judge our present day and the present current of our lives. It must be able to take it all in. Thus, the *end* of fellowship is our Communion's rationale, but only insofar as it judges the difficult shape of our historical life today.

Therefore "God wills fellowship" must understand *will* in terms of command as much as gift. The two must go together. The end of history must judge our obedience within history. That, I suggest, would give us a thicker rationale. Thick rationales engage the actual history of peoples, their struggles for fellowship, and the demands this makes on their capacities and hopes. Anybody who says that communion is straightforward—that it is pretty well established, that it makes no demands on me, and that it does not leave me fundamentally changed in the face of God—is, in other words, working with a thin rationale for communion in the first place. Communion, in such thin versions, looks mostly like one's own self.

※ ※ ※

What might a thick rationale for communion look like, a rationale that takes seriously the thick implications of the 1920 Appeal, founded on the conviction that God wills fellowship?

Let me take up a comment by Ray Aldred, a prominent Indigenous leader and theologian in both church and civil contexts within Canada. Aldred is a member of the Cree Nation, and I recently heard him present a paper relating the Gospel Story (as he calls the larger biblical canon) to Cree indigenous identity: those stories that shape and express Cree understandings of communal life, relationships with the larger world, and the land. Aldred is an evangelical Christian of large interests, and his paper took in theories of narrative and metaphor, the nature of treaty, and the character of relational personhood. It was an extraordinarily rich reflection. One respondent, in the face of Aldred's expansive theory, basically asked: "So Ray, why bother?" Given the destruction that Christian churches and their missionaries and civil culture promoted and visited upon the Cree people, something Aldred engages in painful detail, why try to connect the Cree experience with the Gospel? Why not let these stories go their separate ways? One might rephrase the question in the mode of the present discussion:. Why bother with claims of divine will to fellowship, when clearly that history has failed to play itself out in our midst? Aldred replied, "but you see, I'm a Christian. So I believe the Book of Revelation when it speaks of the time when 'all nations, and kindreds, and people, and tongues' stand before the Lamb's throne and praise him (Rev. 7:9-10). The stories, Cree and Gospel, *have* to come together somehow." More than that, Aldred is willing to say that he has tasted this promise already, although in ways that are not yet resolved or clear. The stories "somehow" *do* come together, he insists, in the form of a gathering of peoples and tongues in this vocally diverse, but devotionally and substantively unified, praise of the Lamb. But they come together with great difficulty.

Much of the intuition behind celebrating our Anglican bonds of affection is inchoately tied to this promise, but it has alas usually been conceived of *minus* the difficulty. If we add that difficulty back in, we get, I suggest, the thicker rationale we have been properly offered. Taking up Aldred's vision of the gathered peoples praising the Lamb, we can point to a kind of Pentecostal rationale behind the Communion's life; but like Pentecost, it has built into it deep and multiple challenges, as the very history behind the great gathering of Revelation implies. Who is this multitude from every nation, John is asked, gathered around the Christ's throne and praising him in every tongue? The elder answers: they are those who come out of the great tribulation, those who have washed their robes in the blood of the Lamb (Rev. 7:9, 13-14). There is, we are told, a history behind this gathering, a rich and bloody history; a thick history.

Indeed, Revelation's promise is the culmination of a set of events laid out scripturally on the day of Pentecost (in Acts 2), a day that sets in motion a deliberate and difficult movement that leads finally to John's heavenly vision. It is not unusual to see Pentecost as the start of some great human gathering across lines of difference. Consider the paeans to the inter-racial character of the Anglican Communion's mission from over a century ago, as at the 1908 Congress. There are versions of this view of God's providence—the Church moves out from narrow Jewish exclusivism to the many-colored coat of the Gospel's cultural multiformity—that end up being extraordinarily thin. Contemporary forms of the bonds of affection rationale usually go this route. But they need not, because the day of Pentecost is actually quite thick.

One can lay out Acts 2 in a straightforward but thickly textured way, and I invite you to follow me for a moment in doing just that. At the start of the chapter, the apostles, now clearly identified and ordered into twelve again by the addition of Matthias, are gathered together. The Holy Spirit comes upon them in a powerful way, visible as fire, with all the destructive holiness the image symbolizes in the Bible. The moment is one of divine crisis. But this critical act of fire falling upon the apostles, bound as it is to judgment and calling, takes the form of preaching in many languages. The apostles now proclaim openly, in the tongues of the nations, "the wonderful works of God": *ta megaleia tou theou.* The phrase is quintessentially psalmic, and appears frequently in diverse vocabulary (see Pss. 40:4; 71:17), tied primarily to two things: the actions associated with God's creative power in making the world, and God's saving of Israel in Exodus (Exod. 15:11) and beyond. A form of the phrase also appears, in an exact way, in the *Magnificat* (Lk. 1:49), where Mary praises "he that is mighty," "who has done great things for me."

We do not know exactly what the wonderful works are that the apostles announced to the crowds. At the least, they must have touched upon the wonders of God's creative power and salvation, much as these were laid out in the Scriptures of Israel and taken up by the Mother of our Lord. At least *this* was announced by the apostles and heard in the many tongues of the nations. I underline the point in passing, but importantly: the Old Testament stands as the opening song to the Gospel's first public proclamation to the peoples of the world, and to whatever final affections before the Lamb they may share. Anglicans have traditionally understood this, though less and less.

To be sure, such proclamation does not yet fulfill the Pentecostal moment that drives forward the Church to Revelation's promised end. The gathered people in Jerusalem of Acts 2 are thrown into a confusion by the recital of divine action from the past, to which Peter responds with an articulate presentation of the "wonderful works of God" accomplished now in the present—a new set of "wonders" (the word Luke uses here is *terata*, a more common one from the LXX). These wonders are associated with God's terrifying re-creation promised by Joel (Acts 2:20), spirit and blood; with Jesus' own miraculous ministry performed in the people's "midst" (2:22); with the magnificent promise of resurrection given to David and now fulfilled in Jesus (2:24); and with his heavenly exaltation (2:25-36). Peter, standing "with the eleven" (2:14), says all this, in what language we are not told. But now, it seems, the borders have all been crossed, as the people "hear" these things in their own language—Parthians, Medes, Egyptians, Arabians, Jews, Greeks. This is what God has done, and "their sound went into all the earth, and their words unto the ends of the world" (Rom. 10:18; cf. Ps. 19:4).

Pentecost is, however, incomplete. The borders have been linguistically crossed, but not yet indwelt. For in response to Peter's words, which culminate in the assertion that "God hath made the same Jesus who ye have crucified both Lord and Christ," the people are "pricked in their heart," sensing that they must do something, troubled that they stand in the face of something whose wonder is fraught also with terror (Acts 2:36-37). "What shall we do?" they ask, to which Peter famously and succinctly responds: "Repent and be baptized in the name of Jesus Christ for the remission of your sins" (2:38). Peter carefully links this call back to the Pentecostal moment of inter-national opening itself. Such repentance, baptism, and forgiveness in Jesus' name, he goes on to say, is itself the threshold through which the Holy Spirit is given, and through which those who are "far off" will be drawn into the promise of Israel's children (2:38-39). These two—pneumatic gift and repentance—go together, as Peter's summary makes clear: "save yourself from this crooked generation" (2:40).

The Pentecostal moment of Acts 2 is *still* not complete, however. Thousands were baptized, we read, and gathered around the apostles in what became, at least for a while, a settled pattern of ecclesial life. As Luke writes of these early believers, they "steadfastly" followed the teaching of the apostles, broke bread, prayed, held all things in common, helped those in need, believed and reached agreement, and praised God in the Temple (Acts 2:41-47). These celebrated verses provided a foundation for later monastic Rules of Life, like those in the Augustinian tradition, with good reason. The life together of the earliest Christians in Acts was bound to the Pentecost moment itself, culminating in "wonders" cascading from God's creation, incarnational self-giving, glorious resurrection and exaltation, and now proclamation to the nations. Thus, we are told that "fear came among every soul; and many wonders and signs were done by the apostles" (2:43). This context of wonder, announced in the languages of every kindred now and later in heaven before the throne of the Lamb, is the pneumatic articulation of apostolic teaching—literally *koinonia*, communion; "fellowship," as the Authorized Version translates.

God wills fellowship. That is, God wills the day of Pentecost and the Pentecostal movement of its promise. God wills it, in the sense that God does it, is doing it, will do it. And God wills it in that we are called to an obedience to just this set of wonderful works, which summon a new force of transformed will.

The works into which our obedience leads, then, will be found along a thick, not a thin, way. And all the talk of Anglican walking together must lead in just this very, very thick *way*. Acts 2, after all, includes apostolic speech, the Scriptures of Israel and their articulation of divine creation, law and redemption, the whole narrative of Jesus, from birth to death to exaltation in Lordship, fear before God, repentance and forgiveness in Jesus' name, a new existence in flight from this present age's wickedness, and the steady centering of life in common teaching, prayer, and material sharing. *All* of this is fellowship or communion, not as a theological abstraction or set of principles, not as a confession or program, but as the historical ordering of the nations to the sacrificial Lamb of God, whose throne stands at the center of everything. All of this embodies, in other words, the bonds of affection that communion expresses. If there is a Pentecostal rationale to the specifically *Anglican* communion, it is one that must follow this entire sweep. Any fellowship that God might will is as thick as this.

There is nothing historically strange in such a claim. The elements of such a thick understanding of fellowship were variously identified and pursued by leaders, laypeople, missionaries, bishops, and others within the multiplying churches that called themselves Anglican well into the 20th century and beyond. But these practical consequences are increasingly forgotten, lost in the scurry and dust of debates. To preach the whole scriptures and stand amazed before the works of God these scriptures present; to trace over and over the form of Jesus that the Gospels lay before us, and recoil in sorrow and fear at our own rebellion and distance from God our Lord; to repent in tears, flee from the distorting claims of a surrounding generation, return to the water of cleansing, and sit at the feet of the apostles in quietness and prayer, so as to share all we have, including the eucharistic supper of the Lamb; and to do so explicitly in the language of and among every people of the earth, so that Jew and Greek, Parthian and Arabian are each and together hearing, repenting, praising, sharing: all this seems to some both too obvious and beside the point in the face of disagreements over sex and doctrine.

Precisely over and against such forgetfulness and disdain are the edges to this form of fellowship. Scripture will be first in this Pentecostal rationale, for the Spirit speaks in the testimony of the Law and Prophets (see Lk. 24:27), that is, the testimony of God's wonderful works, and again and again of Jesus and the descent and ascent that marks his divine life and mission. The Pentecostal rationale presumes Scripture as primary, something that Anglicans understood even before the Communion emerged. This edge cuts against all narrow gospels that would do well to lose themselves in the corridors of our Israelite elders. The nations are brought near by the Spirit in the Scriptures first of all and foundationally.

There is the edge as well, we must avow, of repentance. *What must we do?* the nations ask, struck by the wonders of God announced in the Scriptures. *Repent, be baptized, save yourself from this crooked generation!* The Pentecostal movement that is the ground of fellowship has repentance as its ethical motor, unrelentingly. Repentance is the right side of history. It is always the first and last thing that is said before the mouth can open in praise of God—and even as it speaks. We are indeed pricked to our heart, and driven to our knees, through the Word of God: driven by, with, and for one another.

I want to be clear about the issue of thickness here. A Pentecostal rationale for the Communion will *at least* be evangelistically oriented in a central way, but only at least. It will also be oriented towards a full Scriptural proclamation—not alone, but at least. It will at least be penitential at all moments; at least distinguish itself from surrounding cultures, wheresoever they are; and at least pursue common apostolic teaching, common prayer, and common sharing of goods. Each element is only an *at least* element—absolutely necessary to the Pentecostal movement, but on its own the least of all, the thinnest of all. They must go together. Accordingly, when each becomes its own rationale, communion slips away through their competing claims. Thin rationales give rise to uncontrollable contention. That is where we are today, samid a communion crisis that only mirrors the world's larger human crises. Thick rationales, such as a truly Pentecostal rationale, *contain* contention within the ever textured and converting work of the Holy Spirit. Thick rationales are essential elements of divine conversion itself.

❋ ❋ ❋

My purpose here is not to outline what the Anglican Communion might look like according to a thick Pentecostal rationale. The recent statement from the Anglican-Roman Catholic International Commission (ARCIC) on ecclesiology, *Walking Together on the Way*, gives a taste of what might be involved.[4] The document is deeply in-

---

4 Anglican-Roman Catholic International Commission, *Walking Together on the Way: Learning to Be the Church—Local, Regional, Universal* (London: SPCK, 2018).

terested in structural matters centered on the relation of local, even "regional," and universal forms of Christian life—the nearby and the far away nations, as it were. This is promising because ARCIC ties the "catholicity" of the Church to its missionary center to indicate that the ordering of the Church should express its outward-moving proclamation, and that movement's judgment upon its originating life. Even though the document barely mentions Pentecost, let alone its end point in Revelation 7, it is filled with aspects of those elements I have mentioned from Acts 2: translated witness to the Scriptures, repentance, baptism, salvation, gathering, learning, common prayer, apostolic obedience, sharing of goods. None of these, though, ever rise to the level of rationale itself. *Walking Together on the Way* ends modestly by offering the Anglican Communion a few rather limited and functional structural suggestions, pressing Anglicans to a bit greater universal interest and Catholics to a bit more local focus. For Anglicans, this means the document indicates perhaps a common eucharistic prayer for the Communion as a whole, a common catechism, and more focus and engagement with Canterbury.

However one judges such suggestions, a thicker rationale for communion—and thus a thicker Anglican Communion—must be less timid about taking up such suggestions in the first place. Thick communion will be *eager* to face failures, learn from them, and change, and to develop patience with one another in the process. Such a thick communion will be more grateful for what we have received as God's gifts from both the apostles and the fellowship itself. And it will be more willing to admit in humility, not disdain, that the Pentecostal movement has brought those "far off" into a new place of honor, perhaps greater than those "nearby" (Eph. 2:13). In sum, a thick Pentecostal rationale for communion—any Christian communion—provides a textured setting in which limited proposals like ARCIC's can be engaged, something they would otherwise lack. It does so in at least four ways, and with this I will end.

First, a thick Pentecostal rationale for communion offers a *benchmark for evaluating the current ordered structures* of our particular communion. If God willing fellowship means obedience to *this* Pentecostal movement, then, from a limited Anglican perspective, we can judge—or rather God will judge—our activities and structures accordingly. This would include the next Lambeth Conference; the way the Anglican Consultative Council does its work; the manner of speech, life, and gathering of the Primates; the Archbishop of Canterbury's own words and witness; as well as the commitments of *all* bishops and their clergy, the shape of synods now and in the future, and our formal teaching. The edge of the Pentecostal movement will properly cut *all* of this. While I have argued that our structures emerged out of this movement, it is hardly clear that they are today reflective any longer of its thick identity. But that is something we must assess with fierce honesty in the light of God's will.

Second, a thick Pentecostal rationale provides a *benchmark for evaluating alternative pathways* before Anglicans. Some of ARCIC III's suggestions, such as a common eucharistic prayer and common catechism, fit well with elements of the Pentecostal gathering of apostles in Jerusalem (Acts 2), in terms of prayer and learning. By the same token, it is not clear how ordering Anglican life more centrally around Canterbury fits with or furthers the rationale. But the rationale itself is precisely the place to reflect on these matters. Without it, or something like it, we are left to the vagaries of what is now a dispersed set of competing energies, rather than the Spirit's multi-lingual press toward a univocal acclamation at the Lamb's High Feast.

This leads to a third gift of robust rationale of Pentecostal communion, namely, the *freedom simply to order ourselves anew*. We *are* given both ear and tongue to receive the word of God's great works together. We *are* granted conversion of heart, in their echo, to repent and to change. We *are* offered freshness of vision and act, that we might gather in renewed humility and solidarity. These are not simply claims for a course correction. Such reformation is the *substance* of living in fellowship. I continue to believe that something like the Anglican Covenant, with greater catechetical, missionary, and synodical depth, is a good thing; and that finding a way to integrate and reintegrate protesting bodies like the Anglican Church of North America into the formal Communion is in keeping with the Pentecostal call to repentance and gathering. If I am mistaken in these judgments, it will *not* be because they transgress former habits, or current canons, or settled antipathies. The fellowship God wills is not captive to such restraints. It frees us from them.

Finally, a thick Pentecostal rationale for communion exposes the *ultimately non-Anglican character of the hope for the world's destiny* that drove Lambeth 1920's Appeal in the first place. Communion is not a peculiarly Anglican concern. It is ours only because it is God's for all Christians. Communion, even this struggling Anglican form of it, doesn't belong to us. Because fellowship is God's will in both senses of the term, as God's gift and as God's command, communion can be taken away from some and given to others, as St. Paul makes clear (see Lk. 20:16; Rom. 11:22). It is manifested across Christian traditions, human time, and cosmic promise, and our own obedience is measured only in those far-reaching terms.

In other words, Anglican communion, and "the Anglican Communion," demand *ecumenical transformation*, now more than ever. Lambeth 1920's own discussion of peculiarly Anglican communion was set precisely within an ecumenical context, however limited. The appeal to all of Christendom arose not from arrogance but from the demand of a divine fellowship that far outstripped what the bishops rightly recognized as both struggle and incapacity among Anglicans left to themselves. Lambeth 1920 initiated its call not because Anglicans were better leaders in the Pentecostal movement, but because the movement itself had relativized all leaders, driving all of Jerusalem and the world—Canterbury and Rome, Geneva and Azusa Street—to search for the other. Christians cannot ask who does Pentecost better but only how it happens at all.

Four ways or applications, therefore, of the Pentecostal rationale for communion: present judgment, future possibility, freedom to change, and the wider world's promise. Lambeth 1920 said that this is how God's will *is done* on earth. God has in fact done something and is doing it still. The right side of history, we may say, *has* embraced aspects of our Anglican life, but only as that life has gone beyond itself toward the Lamb's high throne with myriads of others similarly called through the long traversal of Pentecost. The days of a special Anglican charism are probably over, except as a residual set of habits, histories, and relationships. I don't want to dismiss these; they still function in important ways. But we must ask what they are *for*. They are not for specialness itself—special liturgies, special attitudes, special histories, customs, and clothing. They are for getting us somewhere with and for others, in the posture of Jerusalem's impassioned, repentant, self-offering crowds who constituted the world's future. All Christian communion is given, and called forth, for this purpose, and this is just the communion that God wills.

SIX

The Persistent Gift of Episcopacy

James Hawkey

What kind of *appeal*, if any, might the Anglican Communion make to the wider Church Catholic today, one hundred years after Lambeth 1920? We might urge once more that the whole *oikoumene* resound with a strong affirmation of its commitment to full, visible, eucharistic unity. Or again, we might tentatively propose, despite our woes, renewed research around the theme of unity in diversity, taking our own struggles on point as something of a laboratory, the research from which could hold some larger interest.

However, prompted in part by recent discussions in the Church of England, I wish to return to a central point from the 1920 Appeal to All Christian People, namely, its professed confidence that the episcopate is "and will prove in the future to be the best instrument for maintaining the unity and continuity of the Church" (§VII). The

Appeal was correct in its confidence, even if squaring the circle of gift and call in this field of ecclesiology (as in others) requires a lively sense of the both/and of divine providence and human freedom. Commenting in late July 1920 on the revised text of the Lambeth Appeal, Neville Talbot, Bishop of Pretoria, remarked: "If Episcopacy is the mark of a *denomination*, for God's sake let us throw it down."[1] To be sure, episcopacy cannot be the property of one church, if we accept that *apostolicity* names a range of actions to which the Church is called, both in her offices and doctrine. On this count, Catholic-minded ecumenists have, in the long train of the 16th century reformers, sought to commend a historic episcopal office without denigrating the faithfulness and fruitfulness of non-episcopal ministries. Likewise, the Lambeth Appeal (again, at §VII). Following along this line, I want to suggest in this short chapter that Anglicans still have a vocation to share the gift of the historic episcopate with those parts of the Christian family yet to receive it, even as we must seek to discover, learn from, and serve alongside the grace-filled ministries already present in these churches.

The "new call to a wider service" of which the Appeal spoke (§VIII) resonates 100 years on in a different—certainly broader—theological context, downstream of an enormously fruitful ecumenical movement. One remarkable and pertinent fruit has been the research into how episcopacy relates to other expressions of *episcopé* in its personal, communal, and collegial aspects.[2] This point may, in turn,

---

1 Lambeth Palace Library, Bell papers vol 255, fol. 48r, *my emphasis*.

2 See, above all, the landmark convergence text of the World Council of Church's Faith and Order Commission, *Baptism, Eucharist, Ministry*,

be set alongside two other shifts in the discussion, often just below the surface. First, our consciousness of the primacy of the language of *koinonia* when discussing the Church has become much greater.[3] Ecumenical parlance has largely moved from the language of unity to that of communion. The development of a *koinonia* ecclesiology, so fundamental to our dialogues and convergence texts, has enriched not only ecumenical conversation, but also offers fruitful direction for our own internal Communion-wide discussions. It is tempting to attribute the proliferation of this language of *koininia* to the influence of Orthodox theology on the ecumenical movement. But whilst such learning has been profound, we also see developments emerging from within Anglican theology itself, as well as in and since the ecclesiological developments of Vatican II.

The second major shift in theological emphasis I want to note is around the issue of grace. This development is perhaps most famously represented by the Lutheran-Roman Catholic "Joint Declaration on the Doctrine of Justification" of 1999, and by the subsequent association of other global communions with it.[4] But other conversations

Faith and Order Paper 111 (Geneva: WCC, 1982), 26–27, marking a high point of multilateral achievement. Cf. *Episcopal Ministry: The Report of the Archbishops' Group on the Episcopate, 1990* (London: Church House Publishing, 1990); World Council of Church's Faith and Order Commission, *The Nature and Mission of the Church: A Stage on the Way to a Common Statement*, Faith and Order Paper 198 (Geneva: WCC, 2005).

3   See Nicholas Sagovsky, *Ecumenism, Christian Origins and the Practice of Communion* (Cambridge: CUP, 2000).

4   Lutheran World Federation (LWF) and the Catholic Church, "Joint Declaration on the Doctrine of Justification" (1999), available online.

and dialogues have also re-posed the fundamental question of how grace operates in the life of the Church.[5] Several mainline churches now enjoy a broad ecumenical consensus that the communion of the Church is firstly a grace-filled *koinonia*, a participation in the life of the Holy Spirit, before it is anything juridical. Presuming this consensus about justification, we are, as the Joint Declaration notes, in a strong position to explore other topics in its light, including "the relationship between the Word of God and church doctrine, as well as ecclesiology, ecclesial authority, church unity, ministry, the sacraments, and the relation between justification and social ethics."[6]

I don't seek to set up a binary here between law on the one hand and Christology or pneumatology on the other, but rather to emphasize the urgency of tending to our theological environment, and considering questions of faith and order afresh in this context. The—old—Anglican challenge remains to find ways of encouraging other churches to share in the gift of the historic episcopate and thus to renew the visible unity of the Body of Christ. Can we do this in a way that takes seriously the implications of our doctrinal agreements, alongside the theological consequences of how we have learned to describe one another? We can; but not, I think, without tending to two remedial lessons, concerning grace and communion.

---

5   See, e.g., ARCIC II, *Church as Communion*, (1991), available online.

6   LWF and the Catholic Church, "Joint Declaration," 5.43. Cf. the comments by John Gibaut, former Director of Unity, Faith and Order for the Anglican Communion, in "Senior ecumenical panel to discuss Joint Declaration on the Doctrine of Justification," *Anglican Communion News Service* (27 March 2019), available online.

ECUMENICAL GRACIOUSNESS

In 1980, Johann Baptist Metz, the German Roman Catholic theologian and pupil of Karl Rahner, published a book entitled *The Emergent Church*.[7] Metz claims that the question at the heart of the Protestant Reformation—How can we attain to grace?—remains central to the pressing theological and pastoral concerns of all the churches. *Reformation*, in the most positive sense, should be understood as the "restoration of original relationships and connections."[8] Accordingly, Metz argues for a second reformation, in which grace might return to the senses, to freedom, and to politics. Protestantism, he writes, has historically been too detached from the senses. Grace is minimised when we snatch it away from the senses and thereby from the social suffering of humanity.

Those who know Metz will be unsurprised by his subsequent political inferences. He claims that the European Reformation's fear of sin became another kind of fear of contact with the earth and the senses, a fear of bodily social life within which grace is lived. Metz thinks that for many centuries Christianity has been marked by a dualism between the world of grace and the world of the senses. The Protestant reformers' obsession with "pure doctrine" failed to engage with the reality of human life and frailty, leaving it at an abstract level. In this case, Metz believes, grace remains in "the realm of invisibility and intangibility." As we choose to bestow grace upon some and

---

7   Johann Baptist Metz, *The Emergent Church: The Future of Christianity in a Postbourgeois World*, trans. Peter Mann (New York: Crossroads, 1981).

8   *Ibid.*, 50.

withhold it from others, the grace can become "cheap," as something that "does not penetrate our lives but just overarches our earthly-social life."[9] Over against this error, he concludes, we must reunite confessional formulas "with human beings and their praxis."[10]

Applied ecumenically, Metz's analysis can help us root our proposals for greater unity in a grace that is tangible and generous, responding to and imitating the reality of God's transforming action in the various churches of the Church. Taking seriously the practical ramifications of what we have said about one another theologically, we may learn to resist theological caricature. If the Church is herself divine gift, our receipt and subsequent sharing of the gift in turn requires sustained spiritual vigilance. To the point at hand, conversations concerning episcopal order might be transformed by such a generosity, and help to re-calibrate other conversations as well, perhaps producing new priorities.

COMMUNION

The 1920 Appeal was admirably focused and confident in its assertion that "God wills fellowship" (§1). As Professor Radner observes in his chapter here, this means that God wills *koinonia*. Although we think of communion or *koinonia* primarily as a churchly reality—the basic operating system of the Church's life—our churches have also been learning together that *koinonia* is as fundamental to creation as it is

9   *Ibid.*, 55.

10   *Ibid.*, 52.

to redemption.[11] The opening of the World Council of Churches' text on *The Church* refers to the Genesis account of the creation of man and woman as showing how human beings have an "inherent capacity" for *koinonia*.[12] Our reluctance to view it in this way suggests that there is something to Metz's claim that we have developed a fear of "that bodily social life" in which grace is incarnated and celebrated in diverse human communities.

In the Gospels, Christ is the agent of a restored *koinonia* for those who come into his orbit. The Gospels are littered with accounts of how this gift is shared as Jesus moves around. In other words, the sharing of communion can appear mundane, and is never abstract. A few examples from Jesus's own life illustrate this. At his infancy, as the shepherds hurry to Bethlehem, social boundaries are redefined. Jesus pursues an engaged ministry of communion among the outcast, the unclean. He reaches out to women as well as those from the traditional religious establishment who come to him in faith. His touch restores the sick to health. Jesus' own social circle appears to have some degree of practical demarcation, from the inner group of Peter, James and John, to the Twelve and the Seventy; and yet St. Paul's earliest theologising of the Christ event insists that all are one "in Christ" (Gal. 3:28 *et passim*), even as Jesus himself teaches that those who seek to reign with him must be willing to share his suffering. Communion

---

11 Recent work in the International Reformed/Anglican Dialogue is helpful in further exploring this theme.

12 World Council of Church's Commission on Faith and Order, *The Church: Towards a Common Vision*, Faith and Order Paper no. 214 (Geneva: WCC, 2013), I.A.1.

is received and shared on different levels, with differing degrees of intensity, but in the company of Christ it is a gift fundamentally and irreversibly offered for those willing to receive it by grace.

Again, if the primary context of the Church is grace-filled communion with God and one another, we are bound to ensure that what we say about one follows from and reflects this fact.

CASE STUDY

The 2017 report of the Church of England and the Methodist Church in Britain, *Mission and Ministry in Covenant*, proposed to draw both churches into an interchangeability of ministries, and eventually full communion.[13] Having formally recognised one another as "true churches" in the Anglican Methodist Covenant of over a decade ago,[14] and backed up by 40 years of ecumenical work on the succession of faith, *episcopé*, and apostolicity, the report felt prepared to propose a next step: If the president of the Methodist Conference were to receive episcopal ordination, ministers in communion with the president would be able to operate as priests in the Church of England, and vice versa. There would be no re-ordination. According to the plan, there would unavoidably be a relatively short period where some non-episcopally ordained presbyters would operate in the Church of England. This, the report declared, would be "a bearable anomaly" in

---

13   Faith and Order Bodies of the Church of England and the Methodist Church, *Mission and Ministry in Covenant* (2017), available online.

14   "An Anglican-Methodist Covenant" (2013), available online.

the higher cause of the unity of Christ's Church. The proposals, of course, were controversial. Such potential change takes time and demands careful consideration. At the time of writing, still further work will be needed before the proposals return to General Synod.

There is not space here to examine the many arguments of those who felt they could not support *Mission and Ministry in Covenant*, nor should we immediately assume that all the necessary work has been concluded to move forward at speed with the proposals. It is important to note that the Methodist Church in Britain had sought to share in the gift of the historic episcopate without any implied repudiation of a past ministry. Anglicans have been here before, with Reformed Christians in the churches of North and South India, and with Lutherans in the Porvoo Agreement. Methodists and Anglicans share similar understandings of the basic operating systems of ecclesial life. And yet, conversations in the Church of England about *Mission and Ministry in Covenant*, including on the floor of the General Synod, revealed a clash of ecclesiologies, and little consciousness either of the primacy of *koinonia*/communion, or of what Anglicans and Methodists have said together, and about one another, in declarations and dialogue over the last decades. The *koinonia* ecclesiology so beloved of ecumenists and ecclesiologists has not bedded into our local churches. We have not spent sufficient time considering how a methodology of grace might shape such faith and order conversations. Put simply, our theological categories risk not being up to the task ahead. A much greater basic awareness of the twin dynamics of grace and communion would have allowed this conversation to be had in much more fertile and creative ground, testifying to changes in the ecumenical landscape over the last 30 years.

CONCLUSION

How shall we think about this, if we seek—in Metz's terms—to reunite confessional formulas with human beings, communities, and their praxis? In fact, the challenge has something to do with what Dan Hardy called the "'thinkability' of any church in theory and practice." He writes: "It is striking how difficult it is 'to think' any church—its many aspects, relations, and dynamics—and how much more so 'to think' the ecumenical scene, with many churches which vary in all these respects and yet relate to each other in a variety of ways." [15] This is profoundly difficult, made more so by the ongoing diversification of human cultures, the chimera of instant communication, and the introduction of new complexities that appear to further frustrate the unity of the Body of Christ. One hundred years on from the Lambeth Appeal, in situations of global division and Christian fragmentation, it is entirely appropriate to suggest that the gift and unifying sign of the historic episcopate will be of particular value for our time.

At the Fifth World Conference on Faith and Order, meeting in Santiago de Compostela in 1993, Archbishop Desmond Tutu captured something of the frustration over what many felt was systemic ecumenical inertia:

> There are conversations, discussions and plans galore, but hardly anywhere has anything of much significance actually happened. There

---

15 Daniel W. Hardy, "Receptive Ecumenism—Learning by Engagement," in *Receptive Ecumenism and the Call to Catholic Learning: Exploring a Way for Contemporary Ecumenism*, ed. Paul D. Murray (Oxford: OUP, 2008), 430.

have been near-betrothals and engagements but hardly any nuptials, least of all consummations. We have had failed attempts or near attempts. There have been COCU, ARCIC, CUC (in South Africa), conversations between, say, Anglicans and Methodists, Anglicans and Orthodox, Anglicans and Lutherans, Anglicans and Baptists.... Often and again a remarkable degree of agreement or consensus has been reached, and yet, and yet... they have somehow lacked something to propel them to take the logical next step—organic union, becoming one, in any sense that is of significance to their members or to a world looking on with desultory and waning interest. It has seemed that toes have been dipped in the water and then the courage or the will to take the plunge into the stream has failed.[16]

The systemically disjointed, violent, and frequently unjust world of the 21st century is crying out for the unity of the Body of Christ, whether it knows it or not. That world may not always appreciate the theological seriousness of some of the questions Christians ask one another. But Christians must not underestimate the importance of the task if the Church is visibly to be the sign and servant of the coming Kingdom of God. What kind of theological culture might we need to curate in which ongoing and legitimate questions about order and apostolicity can be considered? How might our theological courage be renewed? The Appeal of 1920 reminds us that we must not keep gifts which "rightly belong to the whole fellowship" to ourselves

---

16 "Towards Koinonia in Faith, Life and Witness" in *On the Way to Fuller Koinonia: Official Report of the Fifth World Conference on Faith and Order*, ed. Thomas F. Best and Günther Gassmann (WCC: Geneva, 1994), 96.

(§II). In seeking to share the gift of the historic episcopate with those churches yet to receive it, we must become more conscious both of the insights and theological tools a century of ecumenical dialogue has offered us, and of the primary reality of Christian communities and their praxis. If our ecclesial operating system were more consciously grounded in a methodology of grace and communion, the journey from ecclesiological anomaly to embrace could be understood as a dynamic expression of the *koinonia* which reveals the unity of Christ's body. Churches need structures in order to care for, guard, and nourish the gift of communion. If that communion is truly to be a visible sign of a creation renewed, a first fruit, the task could not be more urgent.

SEVEN

Walking Together, Visibly and Invisibly

Christopher Wells

INTRODUCTION: THE ELUSIVELY UNITARY CHURCH

Presuming, as a matter of faith—inscribed in Holy Scripture, borne by creed and confession—that the Church is somehow one, where may we reliably find it, and how will we know when we do? Ecumenical labor in this field has turned up considerable fruit, by traversing semi-permeable boundaries between the churches of the Church. The bounds are real precisely as our divided denominations perdure, notwithstanding one and another attempt to gather them all together into one visible Whole. At the same time, the bounds are permeable because we have said that we recognize a persistent, real communion of faith and life, given at least in the Scriptures, prayer, baptism in the name of the Trinity, and the saints and martyrs. Many imagine these latter elements, and the institutions that bear them, as together making up the one—visible, or invisible, or both—Church, the singularity of which we maintain by faith, notwithstanding apparent imperfection, impairment, and whatever else prevents our laying hold together of promised fullness. The potential visibility and/or invisibility of the Church remains contested and perplexing.

We find such irresolution in contemporary debates about appropriate means of reform or renovation of structures in the Anglican Communion. The 2009 *Jerusalem Declaration* of GAFCON charts a first approach to the problem by announcing *recognition* of "the orders and jurisdiction of those Anglicans who uphold orthodox faith and practice" (§11). The text attempts to establish or otherwise codify an unimpeachable visibility that right-thinking Anglicans may share and to which they may point. Building on this in its *Letter to the Churches* of 2018, GAFCON's leaders wrote that they "have seen the hand of God leading us toward a reordering of the Anglican Communion." If orthodox Anglicans may be seen, then finding and joining them becomes straightforward, just as other contenders can be exposed as unfaithful frauds. In effect, "nothing is hidden that [has] not been made manifest" (Mt. 8:17).

A second approach to the problem may be found in the *Austin Statement* of the Communion Partner bishops of the Episcopal Church following the General Convention of 2018. The text anchors its argument in a series of ecumenical images, which suggest that the unity of the Church itself, and therefore all the more the unity of Anglicans, may not be so readily apprehensible. To be sure, all

Episcopalians (starting at home) "share the same baptismal identity" and on this basis should seek to "maintain the unity of the Spirit in the bond of peace" (Eph. 4:3) (§2). Walking together in communion, however, is the call of *all* Christians, and the Communion Partners locate their particular vocation within this wider horizon of pilgrimage, the end of which cannot be known (see §5). As they put it: "The larger Church is a catholic whole that includes our brothers and sisters in the Anglican Communion, and indeed Christians all over the world. In the face of crucial differences with our fellow Episcopalians over marriage, we seek the highest degree of communion possible consistent with these commitments" (§6). The ecumenical term of art *degrees of communion* flags a lack of agreed-upon, institutional fullness, while insisting that something real remains. Visibility is relativized, if not foresworn. For now, we may be grateful for "space[s] of differentiation, set within the wider communion of baptism and faith that we continue to share, however imperfectly" (§9).

Is there some way to sort out these varying approaches, perhaps as a contribution to the healing of divisions among Episcopalians and Anglicans more broadly, thence perhaps as a service to the one Church of Christ? There is—and I will alight, at the end of this paper, on a principal grammar upon which Anglicans have settled to describe both the gift and the call of communion under the sign of incompleteness. To show why this solution is compelling, however, I will first repair to the past, to consider how others have sought to hold together the truths of the gospel and the facts of history, including human sin. My Anglican exemplars will be John Jewel and Richard Hooker, but I start with St. Augustine of Hippo (354-430), who stands at the theological source of all western Christian ecclesiology.

In many writings, Augustine's mature teaching about the Church specializes in nuance on the matter of ecclesial location, nuance that all western discussions inherit and appropriate, both for purposes of contestation and negotiation.

AUGUSTINE OF HIPPO, CATHOLIC CATECHIST

A primary and extraordinarily delicate task for Augustine concerned his need to wrench the surviving texts of Cyprian of Carthage (210-258), a great saint of the Church, out of the hands of Donatist misuse. The Donatists were rigorist conservatives who initiated and maintained a breakaway church in Roman North Africa from the fourth century, centered around those who refused to repudiate their faith in the face of persecution. While Cyprian had upheld the unity, visibility, and salvific necessity of the one Church, he had also articulated a middle way between the so-called laxist and rigorist parties of his own day by supporting rebaptism of heretics as a public penance and proof of validity. Against Donatist insistence, the Catholic Church would, in the next century, settle its teaching on this point, aided by Augustine's argument that trinitarian baptism should be deemed valid wherever it takes place, *even as* its salvific effect will not ordinarily kick in unless and until one is reconciled to the Church.

Such a distinction could allow for real sacramental beginnings outside strictly Catholic bounds.[1]

At the same time, Augustine insists with great zeal that simple membership in the visible Church—baptism alone—*also* does not guarantee salvation, since deeper and determinative realities of true holiness and righteousness remain necessarily hidden. This, he says, should be learned from Cyprian. The Church, as described in the Song of Songs, is "a locked garden" and "sealed fountain, a well of living water" (Song 4:12-13). This means that even when sinners—the greedy and fraudulent, robbers, usurers, drunkards, and the envious—"share the same baptism with the righteous, they do not share the same love with them."[2] Thus St. Paul teaches, following an Old Testament precedent, that "a person is a Jew who is one inwardly, and real circumcision is a matter of the heart—it is spiritual and not literal" (Rom. 2:29; cf. Deut. 10:16; Jer. 4:4 and 9:26; Ezek. 44:9). Such spiritually circumcised righteous ones constitute, says Augustine, "the fixed number of the saints predestined before the foundation of the world."[3]

Throwing the Donatists a bone, as it were, Augustine concludes that those who have been baptized "inside" the Catholic Church but who *lack* what St. Peter describes as "the appeal of a good conscience" (1 Pet. 3:21) cannot in fact "belong to the mystery of the ark of which

---

1 See *Augustine through the Ages: An Encyclopedia*, gen. ed. Allan D. Fitzgerald (Grand Rapids: Eerdmans, 1999), 89, 92.

2 Augustine, *On Baptism* V, xxvii, 38. See the new English translation in *The Donatist Controversy I*, ed. Boniface Ramsey and David G. Hunter (Hyde Park: New City Press, 2019).

3 *Ibid.*

Peter speaks." For "how can those who make a false use of holy baptism and continue to the very end of their lives in profligate and dissolute ways be 'saved by water,' even though they may *seem* to be within?" Likewise, recruiting Cyprian to a revisionary end: if those baptized outside the Church later return to it in faith, may we not suppose that "the Lord in his mercy is able to grant forgiveness to them?"[4]

On every count, Augustine's teaching pays practical and pastoral dividends and rebuffs triumphalism.[5] Writ famously as a wrestling with the "mixed body" (*corpus mixtum*) character of the visible Church and her members, Augustine cites Jesus' parable of the wheat and the chaff, which are inseparable for a time until the final winnowing.[6] And he is especially interested in enumerating the several states of sojourning saints both within *and* without the visible Church, to underline the hidden character of God's electing providence. Among the saints, says Augustine, we naturally find the most advanced who *now* "follow the supreme path of love" and are able to instruct others

---

4 *Ibid.* V, xxvii, 39. As Maurice Wiles and Mark Santer note, Augustine quotes Cyprian here to establish "as a rule what Cyprian admitted as an exception." See *Documents in Early Christian Thought*, ed. Wiles and Santer (Cambridge: Cambridge University Press, 1975), 165.

5 In the exposition of Tarsicius van Bavel, the "one Church leads, as it were, two lives and passes through different phases. Therefore the Church in which we now live is not a fixed or completed entity; it is in becoming and in process, in the stage of growing from a mixed body [*corpus mixtum*] into the perfect body of Christ" (173). Accordingly, Augustine is able to describe the Church "in a very realistic way" (172). See van Bavel, "Church" in *Augustine through the Ages*. On "invisibility," see Maureen A. Tilley's entry on *De Baptismo* in *ibid.*, 92.

6 See Augustine, *De doctrina christiana* III 37, 55.

"in a spirit of gentleness." And we also find those persons "still living their lives at the carnal or natural level" who nonetheless fear God, "take great care and trouble to diminish by degrees their love of earthly and temporal things," "give careful study to the rule of faith," and readily accept "the authority of what is catholic." Finally, however, we also find those "still living evil lives, [who] as yet still belong to heretical bodies or even to gentile superstitions. But in their case too, 'God knows those who are his.' For in that ineffable foreknowledge of God, there are many who seem to be outside who are really inside, and many who seem to be inside who are really outside."[7]

In sum, three basic claims found Augustine's teaching on the Church, putting every would-be Christian on notice—on principle, to help inculcate humility. First, the one, *visible* Church consists of those who are baptized and live within her clear bounds, and this institution is the ordinary vehicle for salvation. Second, membership in the Church does not guarantee salvation, since deeper, *invisible* realities are in play. Third, therefore, all Catholic Christians must work out their salvation with fear and trembling—and joy!—neither presuming their own destiny nor that of their invariably insufferable neighbors. They must patiently persevere with others and with themselves in faith, hope, and especially love. This is the promise of the gospel *in* the Church, the two being coextensive.

---

7   All from *On Baptism* V, xxvii, 38.

JOHN JEWEL, CONFIDENT VISIBILIST

I will turn momentarily to Richard Hooker, the oft-heralded architect of Anglican ecclesiology, but John Jewel, Bishop of Salisbury, comes first, having preceded Hooker by a generation and, in fact, served as his patron at Oxford. Hooker would later describe Jewel as "the worthiest divine that Christendom hath bred for some hundreds of years."[8] Be that as it may, it is interesting to ask where Jewel's passionate *Apology of the Church of England* (1562) falls along the Augustinian axis of invisible visibilism. I will attempt to answer by taking seriously Jewel's own constructive theological account, which he offers self-consciously in the teeth of fresh Christian division that demanded uncomfortable inter-ecclesial adjudication.

I say *uncomfortable*, but that may sound moralistic, as if the requisite battle for the Church's purifying ought not call forth, on occasion, a righteous indignation and concomitant courage to answer the enemies of the Church and the gospel. In the latter spirit and with such a purpose in view, Jewel warms to his subject, and his text evinces the frisson of reform, taking the fight to his opponents. For we have, writes Jewel, "put ourselves apart not as heretics are wont, from the Church of Christ, but as all good men ought to do, from the infection of naughty persons and hypocrites"[9]—and more than that,

---

8 Richard Hooker, *Of the Laws of Ecclesiastical Polity* II.vi.4 (hereafter *Laws*). I use the edition in *Works*, vol. 1, ed. John Keble, rev. edn. by R. W. Church and F. Paget (Oxford, 1888).

9 Jewel, *Apology of the Church of England*, Pt. IV; 65. I here cite the pagination in John E. Booty's edition (New York: Church Publishing, 2002).

from the "fellowship" of "men, who, though they be not, yet at least seem and be called Christians."[10] To be sure, these same imposters, having "left nothing remaining in the Church of God that hath any likeness of this Church, *yet will... seem* the patrons and valiant maintainers of the Church," as all heretics always have. Here Jewel notes Arians, Nestorians, Ebionites, and "Mahomites" (or "Saracens"); in an earlier list he includes the Eutychians, Marcionites, Valentinians, Carpocratians, Tatians, and Novatians—in short, "all them which have had a wicked opinion either of God the Father, or of Christ, or of the Holy Ghost, or of any other point of the Christian religion."[11] Curiously, in both lists of heresies, Jewel fails to mention Donatists, the *ecclesial* heretics, whose teaching and actions occasioned St. Augustine's having insisted that the true Church sits secretly within the all-too-visible bounds of a mixed assembly, attended by good and bad Catholic alike. Faced with genuine ecclesiological conundra, the Donatists erred both through premature departure and an embrace of over-realized visibility. In this way, the Donatists occasioned misbegotten division, that is, the very thing prompting Jewel's own writing, amid the ruins of the western Church in his day.

The Augustinian student expects Jewel to acquit Anglicans of just this sinful charge, while at the same time leveling it against his opponents: *they* are the unduly dividing and departing Donatists. That he does not redounds, in part, to his decision to portray Rome not as simply erring—as, therefore, potentially still sitting on the permeable perimeter of the Church, like the Donatists—but rather as itself

---

10   *Ibid.*, Pt. IV; 66.

11   *Ibid.*, Pt. III; 42.

Antichrist. Jewel views Rome as "the very same harlot of Babylon and rout of devils whereof is prophesied so plainly in the Apocalypse."[12] It follows that the Roman church "is severed from the Gospel"—borrowing the phrase, remarkably enough, from St. Cyprian himself.[13]

This suggests a second reason for the absence in Jewel's *Apology* of any real wrestling with Donatism, namely, his not having taken up Augustine's tripartite teaching about the Church as visible, invisible, and mixed. Specifically, the invisibility of the Church has gone missing, subsumed by an unstinting institutionality made to bear the burden of the whole. And with the disappearance of invisibility goes, too, the mediating admission that the one Church suffers unfaithfulness, confusion, and error—even heresy—from within: *sin*, that one day will be rooted out, but not yet.

Bumping into the apparent reality of wheat and tares side by side, just as Jesus promised—for there they are: "this great crop and heap of heresies grow up amongst us"—Jewel declines to draw the dominical conclusion, imagining instead the immediate "vanishing" of heresy once the gospel is permitted properly to shine, like the sun burns off the mist of the morning. As he urges:

> Let [the Roman Catholics] make a proof, let them give the gospel free passage, let the truth of Jesus Christ give his clear light and stretch forth his bright beams into all parts, and then shall they forthwith see how all these shadows straight will vanish and pass

---

12 *Ibid.*, Pt. IV; 74.

13 *Ibid.*, Recap.; 137.

away at the light of the gospel, even as the thick mist of the night consumeth at the sight of the sun.[14]

Reading Jewel charitably, as we must, he seems not so much anti- as pre- or simply non-Augustinian. Irenical perorations on the mixed body and the necessary hiddenness of the city of God may be spoken of again anon. For now, the Church herself must be re-set, re-initiated, as Jewel says, "upon a high and glistering place, in the top of an hill (see Isa. 2:2), and built upon the foundation of the apostles and prophets (see Eph. 2:20)."[15] And the Church *has been* so restored, he insists, as may be seen not merely by baptism as a public marker of membership but also by a demonstrable holiness of the faithful, since "God hath plucked us out 'from the power of darkness, to serve the living God' (Rom. 8:11), to cut away all the remnants of sin...; that it may *appear* how... the Spirit of sanctification is in our bodies and... Christ himself doth dwell in our hearts."[16] Sanctification, the usually-long process of Christian perfecting that, please God, may issue in the salvation of one's soul—at the end of the pilgrim journey—is here presented as a kind of souped-up baptism, comparably public and susceptible of scrutiny.

Jewel's dogged focus on differentiation is understandable in the context of defending the Church of England's recent re-structuring, with henceforth no ecclesial or juridical overlap with the Roman Catholic world: a clean break. But his portrait of the one Church, or

---

14   *Ibid.*, Pt. III; 43.

15   *Ibid.*, Pt. IV; 76.

16   *Ibid.*, Pt. II; 39.

his own church, as they are in Christ and in history is innovative by traditional standards, that is, mistaken. In a bid to raise the bar on a sullied, cultural Christianity with too-little verve, Jewel proposes in its place a hopefully reformed Christianity no less culturally embedded with wildly inflated expectations for verifiable success, *pace* both tradition and Scripture (cf. Heb. 12:1).

RICHARD HOOKER, PRINCIPLED PLURALIST

Thirty years hence, locked in hand-to-hand combat with the Puritans, Richard Hooker approaches these questions differently in his monumental *Laws of Ecclesiastical Polity* (1594), a text that has remained foundational for Anglican thinking about the Church. Downstream of the first generation of Anglican Reformers, Hooker cannot simply evoke the corruptions of Rome and stipulate the authenticity of the nascent Church of England. Following any period of institutional upheaval must come a time of reconstruction and reordering, and careful, well-communicated thought is necessary if reforms are to be received. For Hooker, this meant setting the Church of England within a wider, recognizably catholic ecclesiology, at once ancient and accountable to the cultural constraints of English society, subject to the crown. He presents, therefore, a Church of England as the normal vehicle of Christian formation in one place, properly *established* to this end, over against other contenders—not only Rome but also Geneva in Puritan guise. In this way, Hooker paints on a larger canvas than Jewel, and bequeaths to Anglicans, even outside England, a set of questions that remain unavoidable.

Seeing a need for maximal breadth, Hooker repairs to Augustine in order to ask and answer the primary, pre-denominational question of the nature of the one Church, her character and features. First and fundamentally, says Hooker, the Church is a single "body mystical" that incubates would-be disciples who seek to develop a sound and sincere love that comes, in the words of St. Paul, from "a pure heart and a good conscience and a faith unfeigned" (1 Tim. 1:5). At this level, the Church is hidden and *invisible*, a mystery, and only God can pronounce on the state of each person. At the same time, the Church has duties, and here we pass into the realm of *visible* verifiability, what Hooker calls "a sensibly known company." This "visible Church" is likewise singular, and enjoys moreover a "uniformity" of faith, as all her members, according to Scripture, profess one faith, one Lord, one baptism.[17]

Thirdly, however, simply naming our belief in Christ does not prove us to be Christians "unless we also embrace that faith," and here Hooker comes to the ineluctable *mixture* within the visible Church. For many who profess faith in Christ are "impious idolaters, wicked heretics, persons excommunicable, yea, and cast out for notorious improbity." They in fact do not belong to Christ's mystical body. Thus, our Lord compares the Church on earth to a field, writes Hooker, where "tares manifestly known and seen by all men do grow intermingled with good corn, and even so shall continue till the final consummation of the world. God hath had ever and ever shall have some [such] Church visible upon earth." We find this in the Old Testament, as well,

---

17 All from *Laws* III.i.1-2; 338-39.

wherein the "people of God" wend their way through calf worship, brazen serpents, the gods of other nations, Baals, and on and on. But because they retained "the law of God and the holy seal of his covenant," they remained "the sheep of his visible flock…, even in the depth of their disobedience and rebellion."[18] Likewise, where St. Cyprian's second Council at Carthage (in 256) supposed that "baptism administered by men of corrupt belief" could not be accounted as a sacrament, the Nicene Council would come to a different conclusion. On all counts, Christians must be prepared to adjudicate between "parts of the Church," concludes Hooker, recognizing that from the beginning, each has not always been "equally sincere and sound." Thus, Judah is more faithful than Israel; or, in St. Paul's time, the church in Rome has more integrity than those in Corinth and Galatia.[19]

Christians in the Church of England certainly *hope*, writes Hooker, "that to reform ourselves, if at any time we have done amiss, is not to sever ourselves from the Church we were of before. In the Church we were, and we are so still." But this must be true of others, as well—the Lutherans, for instance, and even the Church of Rome, with which the Church of England can still seek to "hold fellowship," insofar as it "lawfully may."[20] And here Hooker comes to a fascinating point, drawing the opposite conclusion of his Puritan interlocutors—and of Jewel:

---

18   *Ibid.*, III.i.5-8; 340-43.

19   *Ibid.*, III.i.9; 344 (cf. 345).

20   *Ibid.*, III.i.10; 346-47.

Even as the Apostle doth say of Israel that they are in one respect
enemies but in another beloved of God (Rom. 11:28), in like sort
with Rome we dare not communicate concerning sundry her
gross and grievous abominations, yet touching those main parts
of Christian truth wherein they constantly still persist, we glad-
ly acknowledge them to be of the family of Jesus Christ; and our
hearty prayer unto God Almighty is, that being conjoined so far
forth with them, they may at the length (if it be his will) so yield
to frame and reform themselves, that no distraction remain in any
thing, but that we "all may with one heart and one mouth glori-
fy God the Father of our Lord and Saviour" (Rom. 15:6), whose
Church we are.[21]

Hooker has traveled some distance beyond St. Augustine's more
clearly demarcated end point—to wit, return to the Catholic Church
that you may be saved. Perhaps he has even wandered off the path,
insofar as Hooker imagines, as Augustine did not, the possibility of
multiple parts of the Church sharing a common identity and location
in the one body. Hooker's picture is biblical, however, displaying and
commending pursuit of unity with other Christians in other places
and jurisdictions, to the extent that we see ourselves as bound to them
in a single family, as he says. Moreover, since we share the "main parts
of Christian truth,"[22] we all may seek the same end, albeit by various
means in sundry locales. In each of these ways, Hooker presumes
and applies the Augustinian dialectic of visibility and invisibility, set

---

21   *Ibid.*, III.i.10; 346-47.

22   *Ibid.*, III.i.10; 347.

within a horizon of God's sure sifting and just judgment. A principled, historically verifiable permeability has appeared around the edges of the Church, which consists of plural churches—each given a name "betokening severalty, as the Church of Rome, Corinth, Ephesus, England, and so the rest";[23] each, therefore, reckoned to be a *reputable* "part of the house of God" and "limb of the visible Church of Christ," as he will say later, in direct reference to Rome.[24]

There are questions here for Anglicans certainly, and for ecumenical Christians thinking along similar lines, including Roman Catholics who may note resonances *avant la lettre* with Vatican II's account of a singular Church incorporating multiple *communitie*s. If "the Catholic Church is ... divided into a number of distinct societies, every of which is termed a church within itself," as Hooker finally concludes,[25] how to make sense of overlapping denominations in single geographic areas?—Anglicans, Presbyterians, Lutherans, Catholics, and many others, ensconced cheek by jowl in most corners of the world; denominations that, moreover, stretch round the world in would-be global fellowships, including an "Anglican" communion notionally centered around but no longer confined to England, something Hooker could not have foreseen.

In this case, do the various churches function as merely *ecclesial* societies, inculcating distinct denominational mores and byways? Is our task simply to cultivate peculiar Christian subcultures, perhaps increasingly introverted and introspective, or otherwise competitive

23 *Ibid.*, III.i.14; 352.

24 *Ibid.*, V.lxviii.9; 375.

25 *Ibid.*, III.i.14; 351.

with one another, like so many brands, left to market themselves? If so, *society* will have lost much of its missionary richness, evoking as it did for Hooker deep encounter with place, hence history, language, regional sins, and much more.

Similarly, what of the visible Church in such a situation? Will it have gone into hiding? Indeed, in an ecumenical age, how can various churches seeking to sing off the old Augustinian song sheet imagine that they are somehow working together, and so faithfully profess one Lord, one faith, one baptism? With so much water under the bridge since the 16th century, what is the state of the Una Sancta today, where may she be found, and how might Anglicans, among others, serve her?

CATHOLIC VISIBILITY SHARED BY ALL

It should be clear that the visibility of the one Church is basic to her identity, and so must never be surrendered, set aside, or forgotten. From the beginning, Christians have seen rising around them a singular, God-given, God-formed Church, sent out like Israel with transformative good news to share with the nations. "This is the Lord's doing, and it is marvelous in our eyes" (Ps. 118:23). To be sure, Jesus advises, "let your light shine before others" (Mt. 5:16). We have some agency in the Church; we are called to protect and propagate the faith and to take counsel. But first and finally the one Church is Christ's own body, and the Holy Spirit will not be stifled. All tribes and peoples, and "all things, whether on earth or in heaven," *will* witness the Pentecostal illumination of the Church. God in Christ *is* "making peace through the blood of his cross" (Col. 1:20). The promise is for the Jew first, but then "for all who are far away, everyone whom the Lord our God calls to him" (Acts 2:39).

In this providential, pneumatic light, the existential questions for Christians and churches in every time and place are: *Where* is the Church, *what* is her mission, and *how* may I share in it? Our ability to answer is complicated by besetting divisions, both between and within our churches—one proof of the *mixed body* character of the Church. But the vocation to visibility is not thereby abrogated.

The bishops gathered at the Lambeth Conference of 1920 grappled with this problem and left an influential record of their work, writ in a series of appropriately visual images. Adopting "a new point of view," namely, "to look up to the reality as it is in God," the bishops saw that "the one Body exists. It needs not to be made, nor to be remade, but to become organic and visible." By this they envisioned not a "uniform" Church but an appropriately diverse "fellowship of one visible society whose members are bound together by the ties of a common faith, common sacraments, and a common ministry." Beyond "vague federation," therefore, and beyond the "self-will, ambition, and lack of charity" that have led to the "sin of disunion," such a reunited Body could, "so far as this world is concerned," show forth the "fulness of Christian life, truth and witness." This, the bishops concluded, "is what we mean by the Catholic Church."[26]

---

26 "Encyclical Letter" of Lambeth Conference 1920, in *The Six Lambeth Conferences 1867–1920*, ed. Randall Davidson (London: SPCK, 1929), Appendix, 12; Resolution 9 §1 and 9 §3 (= the Appeal), available online.

The state of the question of the Church's visibility has hardly changed in the intervening century, save in the unleashing of great ecumenical energies that re-made most churches, including the Anglican Communion. We Christians know what to do. We are called by God to "gather up the fragments, so that nothing may be lost" (Jn. 6:12). This is, in fact, old-fashioned Augustinian ecclesiology in the key of patience and penitence.

THE INESCAPABILITY OF COUNSEL

With St. Augustine and Richard Hooker, following our Lord, we cannot forget that the Church's perfect unity, holiness, catholicity, and apostolicity are not apparent on this side of glory, as a divine accommodation to human sin and a divine goad to sanctification. Jesus says, "by their fruits, ye shall know them" (Mt. 7:16) and also: "Let both [the weeds and the wheat] grow together until the harvest; and at harvest time *I* will tell the reapers..." (Mt. 13:30). Thus, *God* forms the pilgrim faithful over time, those who are called and given grace to persevere to the end, and God will render final judgment. In such a setting, many Christian communities would do well to understand their life together as "transitional," in the imaginative term of the 1930 Lambeth Conference.[27] We are all waiting for more to be given—revealed and enacted—by God at the proper time. We will want

---

27 *The Lambeth Conference 1930: Encyclical Letter from the Bishops with Resolutions and Reports* (London: SPCK, 1930), Report IV on "The Anglican Communion," 153.

to remain attuned to flexible forms of communion, both for ourselves and for the sake of others, in order to steward what we receive.

Given that our present disarray is, we trust, a way station en route to something better, how can we imitate today Christ's having broken down the wall of division between Jew and Gentile "that he might create in himself one new humanity in place of the two, thus making peace" (Eph. 2:14,15)? What next steps will help us advance in faithfulness as Christ's members made into "one body through the cross" (Eph. 2:16)? Such questions invoke the sacrificial character of ecclesial life in service of visibility as well as discernment about the fullness of the Church's witness.

We Anglicans and others, who share a common baptismal faith across the numerous churches of post-16th-century western Christianity, need a field guide for adjudicating visibility and invisibility amid division. There can be no escaping counsel, that is, constant communication and consultation, which may take various forms, including traditional councils, synods, and so forth. As the bishops gathered at the 1930 Lambeth Conference reflected, perhaps their own decennial meeting "with its strict adherence to purely advisory functions has been... preparing our minds for participation in the Councils of a larger and more important community of Churches. Every extension of this circle of visible fellowship would increase the power of the Church to witness to its Lord by its unity."[28] And since the members of the body *cannot* say to each other "I have no need of you" (1 Cor. 12:21), they must likewise face each other in love when hard things need to be said (see Paul's confrontation with Peter at Gal.

28 *Lambeth Conference 1930*, "Encyclical Letter," 29.

2:11; cf. Eph. 4:15: "speaking the truth in love"). For Augustinian heirs, a critical question will be: How can our common counsel account for the hidden aspect of the Church, her God-ordained invisibility, and so proceed with proper reserve? How can we leave to God that which is God's, while at the same time discerning, in St. Paul's terms, the difference between sad-but-necessary *divisions* and salutary *diversity* (see 1 Cor. 11:19 and 1 Cor. 12:12ff.)? According to the apostle, each has its place, but they are not the same. The ancient and correct answer is: by the Church's own gathering and deciding.

IMPERFECT COMMUNION ACROSS DISTANCE

Here, finally, we should sharpen the immediate challenge before Anglicans. Seeking to respond to the call of international communion, we have said for over a century that "intensified" life together is more faithful than federation.[29] Unless we wish to renege on that vision so as to recast the Communion in a new image—either as relentlessly federalist, or in would-be post-Canterbury guise—our questions will concern the model of intensification and its timeline. Here, I see two proposals on the table, both covenantal in character.

---

29 See "Report VII" of the Committee Appointed to Consider Relation to and Reunion with Other Churches in *The Six Lambeth Conferences 1867–1920*, Appendix, 132: "For the manifold witness of the Church would be intensified and extended beyond all measure if it came from an undivided Society of Jesus Christ." Cf. Anglican Covenant (2009), Intro. §5, available online.

Convened in 2016 by the 6th Global South Conference, a study group "on enhancing ecclesial responsibility" delivered a draft "covenantal structure" to the 7th conference meeting in Cairo in October 2019, which adopted it.[30] The text is full of scriptural and historical riches and deserves careful study. Building on the 2011 report of the Inter-Anglican Standing Commission on Unity, Faith and Order, *Toward a Symphony of Instruments* (2012), the proposed structure seeks to advance Anglican coherence first of all in a global south context, but with an eye to wider application "for the well-being of our Anglican Communion."[31]

From a classical perspective, the call for wider counsel and decision-making about the Church concerning controverted matters rings true. Hooker, and successive Lambeth conferences, would concur. The readiness of the text to set aside "mere geographical location," however, so as to isolate pockets of putative "orthodoxy" signals an over-realized visibilism without qualification, hence without needed restraint.[32] Who, for instance, will determine when a given bishop's *jurisdiction* has become "unintelligible" and "inauthentic"?[33] Likewise, was the 1552 text on *The Reformation of Ecclesiastical Laws* (cited by the Global South authors) correct when it supposed that "the coming

---

30 *A Covenantal Structure for the Global South Fellowship of Anglican Churches*, adopted 11 Oct. 2019, updated 15 Oct. 2021; available online at www.thegsfa.org.

31 *Ibid.*, Executive Summary 3.iv.

32 *Ibid.*, Executive Summary 4.i.

33 *Ibid.*, 1.6; cf. 2.1.6

together of all faithful men" is a matter that may be "perceived"?[34] John Jewel would agree, but only by way of dispensing, as we saw, with the invisibility of the Church, thus also with her mixed body character, incorporating even heretics, as Hooker allowed. In this revisionist conception, communion becomes an all-or-nothing matter, either "full" or absent, as the text apparently concludes.[35] *Degrees* of faithfulness, so helpful in the pedagogy of communion for distinguishing real progress from *all* that we are called to, are removed from the inter-Anglican ecclesiological toolbox.[36]

The Anglican Covenant avoids these errors by channeling received ecumenical thinking about the Church—that communion is baptismal in the first instance; that even among Anglicans it is both "beauty and challenge;" and that, because there's more to the Anglican family than meets the eye, we pray (in the subjunctive, of course), that God "will redeem our struggles and weakness" and "renew and enrich our common life."[37] This is a reformed summons for an ever-reforming Church. In turn, each section of the Covenant presents a gift and call structure. Affirmations lead to complementary commitments, finally regarding the form of "interdependent life" itself.[38] When "situations of conflict" arise, "face to face meetings, agreed parameters, and a willingness to see such processes through" are prescribed, in a bid "to

---

34 *Ibid.*, Executive Summary 6.

35 *Ibid.*, 2.1.6.

36 Cf. *ibid.*, 2.2.3(b).

37 *The Anglican Communion Covenant*, Intro. §§1-3, 4, 8; see more fully 2.1.3. The text is available online.

38 *Ibid.*, 3.2.

uphold the highest degree of communion possible."[39]

The "relational consequences" of section four of the Covenant[40] were underdeveloped and perhaps broadly conceived as a kind of social distancing, in current parlance, when what we actually need is physical distancing in truth and love. Call it "walking together at a distance," as Archbishop Welby described a 2016 decision of the primates.[41] When we disagree on matters of importance without a ready solution at hand, some means of honoring the faith we still share without piling on expectations of fullness can be both attractive and coherent. We do this all the time with ecumenical partners, as with family members. Communication is maintained and cooperation encouraged, even as some slackening of business as usual is reluctantly accepted as an outworking of freedom and respect. In this way, boundaries may become byways that prepare the passage of pilgrims still learning how best to "wait for one another." When we do "come together" again, we hope "it will not be for our condemnation" (1 Cor. 11:33,34).

Let us pray that Anglicans of all parties and persuasions may at least not seek to prevent the developing of structures for common discernment, so long as these structures also enable patient endurance (2 Cor 1:6, Col. 1:11, Jas. 5:10-11; cf. Heb. 10:36-39). Duly marking the great mystery of our having died in baptism, through which we were "hidden with Christ," let us labor to build up the body in every

---

39   *Ibid.*, 3.2.6-3.2.7.

40   *Ibid.*, 4.2.4, 4.2.7.

41   Gavin Drake, "ACC commits to 'walking together' with the Primates," *Anglican Communion News Service* (April 20, 2016).

good work, until the life of each one is "revealed with him in glory" (Col. 3.3,4). Walking together, even at varying paces, we can, please God, look together to Christ, who is first and last, and himself the *way* upon which the Church is drawn. *He will come again to judge the living and the dead.*

EIGHT

More Catholic Catholicity

Fellowship as God Wills

Jeremiah Yang Guen Seok

INTRODUCTION: REMEMBERING THE 1920 APPEAL

Conflicts over hegemony between the nations within Europe caused the First World War. In this imperial power struggle, nine million people were sacrificed. In the aftershock, the "Appeal to all Christian People" of Lambeth Conference 1920 marked an Anglican attempt to take responsibility. In the Appeal, Anglicans demonstrated a deep understanding of the causes of the war, stoked in part by the long-standing division and conflict among Christian churches.

Through the Appeal, Anglican bishops in 1920 called for the restoration of catholicity and visible unity. The Appeal expressed an admirable humility in a bid to hear God's call amid crisis. The bishops recognized that they were called to strive for the realization of ecclesial catholicity through the fellowship of divided churches. Such fellowship would be an example for the healing of wounds and the reconciliation of conflicts caused by the war.

In other resolutions of the same conference, the bishops made a sincere and concrete call for a new relationship and new international order based on the catholicity of the gospel of Christ. Both for divided churches and divided nations and peoples, the bishops expressed hope for new relationships and new order. They urged all churches to support the recently formed League of Nations (resolutions 3-6, 78). The League presented a narrow channel that at least introduced liberation and independence for colonized nations and peoples. In all of these ways, the 1920 Lambeth Conference modeled an ecumenical mind and ecumenical program for all Anglicans, aimed out to the whole Church and world.

As Anglican bishops continue to gather more than 100 years on, what is our understanding of the present crisis of the world? What is God's calling for Anglicans living in a time when divisions and conflicts are again intensified, even as the survival of earthly life is threatened? Can we make a new ecumenical and catholic Appeal in this situation? If so, what form might it take?

CRISES OF OUR TIME

The present global political situation closely resembles that of the early 1910s. Isolationism has been strengthening, and struggles for hegemony between imperialist powers or power blocks have become increasingly intensified. Political attempts to form hegemonic allied forces or power blocks are evident. Emperor-like rulers have emerged at the apex of political leadership in all the continents. This power struggle unsettles present international order and abandons the minimum amount of compassion that past orders showed. These powers' attitude toward weak countries and peoples are bluntly high-handed and violent. Economic exploitation disguises itself as the demand for equal relationship in the rhetoric of empires. Shameless naked military intimidation is legitimized in the name of freedom and democracy. In this situation of imperial hegemonism and isolationism, weak and poor people are struggling to survive on small ferry boats that carry refugees to camps and along borders between concrete walls. In point of fact, we are in a warlike situation in which unaccountable numbers of lives are being sacrificed in all parts of the world.

Concerns have been expressed about extreme relativism in the world of globalization and pluralization. Even in the diagnosis of difficulties occurring within the Anglican Communion, there have been warnings against the abuse of autonomy easily turning to unlimited relativism. But as I see the situation, the reality is more complicated. Remorseless hegemonism and isolationism dangerously imperil life on the earth, turning it into a battlefield ruled by the law of the jungle and "winner take all." Relativism *and* hegemony, therefore, have conspired together from the beginning. In neo-liberal market capitalism, we see an irresponsible bending of truth in service of strong power. In order to distort and manipulate the freedom toward truth and love into the freedom of desiring and possessing unlimitedly, everything becomes relativized and all living beings changed into objects to be possessed. For this ruthless relativization, oppression, and violence are necessary because the relativism is realized by separating everything from living human relationships. In such a manner, freedom and violence, relativism and monopoly, are very often in a relationship of complicity. And from this complicity, the freedom to ignore, stigmatize, exclude, hate and, attack is encouraged in the support of militarism and violence.

According to Indian theologian Christopher Duraisingh, "what is needed is a rejection of *both* the postmodern radical relativism and its notion of incommensurability of cultures *as well as* the Enlightenment claims for all-encompassing and ahistorical meta-framework and universals."[1] I would like to consider, however, the complicity of freedom and violence as well as relativism and monopoly, rather than view them as separate issues. As I understand it, this pertains to the fundamental nature of the present crisis of this world. It is also the most serious threat to the unity and catholicity of the Christian Church. The complicity is based on the distorted secular understanding of important ecumenical concepts like unity, catholicity, the relationship between unity and diversity, and the relationship between autonomy and communion. And our churches live under

1   Christopher Duraisingh, "Contextual and Catholic: Conditions for Cross-Cultural Hermeneutics," *Anglican Theological Review*, 82/4 (Fall 2000): 679, emphasis added.

the rule of these distorted understandings of unity and diversity, catholicity and locality. Therefore, we can say that the crisis of this time is very much the crisis of unity and catholicity.

In my context, the various rhetorics of reconciliation produced in the celebration of the 500th anniversary of Martin Luther's Reformation in 2017 were not very well accepted. Although there were several events to remember Martin Luther and to reexamine his theology of justification, there were very few opportunities to share the history of Reformation with Korean society. For me and my colleagues, the threefold "not for sale" (Salvation: Not for sale; Human beings: Not for sale; Creation: Not for sale) touched our heart more than any other words, stories, and events for the reconciliation of divided church families. As the Lutheran World Federation webpage introduces them, these themes "capture a key insight that triggered Luther's public opposition to ecclesial practice of his time."[2] They not only show an honest understanding of the crisis of Church and world today but also suggest the right direction for the realization of unity and catholicity. All ecumenical dialogues and efforts to reconcile divided churches should be expressed as a common effort in a true fellowship to discern the crisis of our time, to hear God's call, and to decide missionary practices, in the hearing of others' voices. In Korea, we hope that the pursuit of unity and catholicity can be extended into deeper and wider dimensions of our life than the healing of wounds made by the division of churches in Europe. We think that

2 "Salvation, Human Beings and Creation — Not for Sale," Liberated by God's Grace: Twelfth Assembly of The Lutheran World Federation, available online.

the threefold "not for sale" is closer to the more catholic catholicity we would like to see.

The threefold "not for sale" witnesses to the extent and depth of marketization, commercialization, and commodification. These forces are now reaching not only into the deeper dimensions of the human spirit but also into outer space. The great cultural and spiritual heritages of humanity are being separated from their proper heirs to be commodities in the market rather than common resources for humanity. Everything in the world is regarded as a possible commodity satisfying selfish human desires, rather than as a partner sharing our earthly life or as challenging us and inviting us to new relationships beyond our own boundaries. This totalitarian domination of a commercial world view is itself a distorted vision of unity and catholicity.

According to the report released by the Intergovernmental Panel on Climate Change (IPCC) following its meeting in Incheon, Republic of Korea, on 1-5 October 2018, the crisis caused by such a distorted vision of unity and catholicity is not likely to allow enough time to begin again.[3] It warns us of the apocalyptic impact the projected climate change would have on humanity, and that there is not much time left to avert it. The critical moment at which human efforts cannot work anymore for the prevention or delay of the coming of catastrophe is very close. António Guterres, UN secretary general, said: "If we don't urgently change our ways of life, we jeopardise life itself. My generation has failed in its responsibility to protect our

---

3 "Global Warming of 1.5°C," IPCC, available online.

planet. That must change."[4] According to the IPCC's report, the time span left for us is only 10–20 years. The outlook for our planet's life is very dark. The Swedish activist Greta Thunberg's biting prophetic rebuke cannot be avoided: "Yet you all come to us young people for hope: how dare you? You have stolen my dreams and my childhood with your empty words. And yet I'm one of the lucky ones. People are suffering. People are dying. Entire ecosystems are collapsing. We are in the beginning of a mass extinction, and all you can talk about is money and fairy tales of eternal economic growth. How dare you!"[5] Christians' efforts to reunite and to realize the catholicity of the Church can not escape from this prophetic rebuke, in view of the results so far achieved. This is the situation of crisis in which we have to reexamine the meaning of unity and catholicity and hear it again from God. I wonder whether we avoid the most dangerous threats to unity and catholicity and settle for the present framework of ecumenical dialogue. We need to strip ourselves of false securities and open ourselves to those who desperately want reconciliation, fellowship, and the catholicity of God's love.

---

4   António Guterres, "Remarks at 2019 Climate Action Summit," delivered September 23, 2019, at the United Nations; available online.

5   "Transcript: Greta Thunberg's Speech at the U.N. Climate Action Summit," available online.

RE-FRAMING ECUMENICAL DIALOGUE

In the early 1900s, it was possible to reduce the problems in the world to the conflicts among imperial powers. The fate of colonized peoples in other continents lay in the hands of empires. The competition among colonial empires decided the future of individuals and communities. Many of the issues for Christianity in the mission fields related to the influence of division and competition between the European churches. Yet I am suspicious about the continued application of such a colonial framework for understanding the crisis of our own time and discerning God's missionary calling. Is it still true that most of problems threatening the unity and catholicity within and without the Church, particularly in the Global South, have been caused by the European history of church division? Even in Europe, is it true that those conflicts and problems correspond to the old denominational division lines? As I see it, most of the divisions and conflicts seriously threatening the unity and catholicity of the Church are taking place traversing a given communion or a community. Not only the conflict between the north and the south, but also the conflict within the south and within the north is more serious now. The content and nature of the crisis is very different from the 1920s. Here, again, we need to ask whether the present framework by which we analyse the crisis is still appropriate. How helpful is our view of unity and catholicity, based on the vision of reconciliation among European churches divided in the Reformation period, for the reconciliation of peoples and communities in the suffering of conflict today? I do not say that the history of Church division and the effort to reconcile those divided churches are neither important nor relevant to present conflicts within Church and society. In order to respond faithfully to the present crisis explained above, however, we need a more catholic and more missionary framework than the one depending on the history of the past division.

In fact, the demand for a more catholic understanding of the catholicity of the Church has been continuing in churches in Asia and other continents outside of Europe since the 1960s. This demand for a new understanding of catholicity is related to the decolonialization of theology and mission. In the continued discussions on inculturation or contextualization and on the catholicity and locality of churches, a new understanding of catholicity has been developed.

For example, as Aloysius Pieris writes, the mission crisis of the Asian church is an "authority crisis" rather than an identity crisis.[6] For him, the crisis of authority is the crisis of credibility. The crisis comes from the fact that the church in Asia has not become "a new credible symbol of God's saving presence among our peoples," "an authoritative word from a source of revelation universally recognized as such in Asia," and

> a new missionary community truly qualified to announce God's kingdom and mediate the liberative revolution inaugurated by Jesus through his life and death — that is, a community that seeks no other sign of credibility and authority than that which such mediation would bestow upon it.[7]

---

6   Aloysius Pieris, *An Asian Theology of Liberation* (London: T&T Clark, 1988), 35.

7   *Ibid.*, 35-36.

The local churches in Asia have remained the branches or outposts of churches in the West. They have failed to fulfil their mission and to produce local churches of Asia. In fact, this crisis of authority and credibility is the crisis of ecclesiology and the catholicity of the Church, because it is coming from the failure to witness God's love for the whole. Therefore, according to Pieris, what is needed for acquiring credibility is "an ecclesiological revolution."[8]

The way proposed by Pieris to instigate an ecclesiological revolution is very instructive for our reflections on unity and catholicity. It does not mean simple inculturation. It is not a simple assertion that the churches in Asia should be culturally and religiously inculturated churches in order to be able to evangelize Asians. For him, the witness of catholicity is prior to inculturation:

> Neither textual proofs (our authority is mentioned in our holy books) nor the appeal to tradition (we always claimed this authority and people used to accept it) are adequate today. *Authority is the spontaneous manifestation of a church's competence to mediate total liberation for the peoples of Asia.*[9]

Here, the competence to mediate total liberation for the peoples of Asia is about ecclesial catholicity.

Pieris' ecclesiological revolution is about becoming a truly local and catholic church of Asia. The first and foremost priority for this revolution is the missionary commitment to witness the catholicity

---

8   *Ibid.*, 35.

9   Pieris, *Asian Theology*, 37; italics in original.

of the gospel. Inculturation and denominational identity are accompanied by the missionary commitment. What is inferred from his understanding of ecclesiological revolution, as I see it, is both the refusal of relativism and of hierarchical monopoly or unity. Catholicity cannot be revealed through the hierarchical unity in which the Church on earth is understood as God's colony and churches in other continents are regarded as the sub-colonies. Catholicity will come through the missionary commitment to witness God's love for all people in the world. In that catholic mission, autonomy cannot be relativism, unity cannot be uniformity, and one local church cannot monopolize the catholicity of the one holy Church. A local church will become an authentic and responsible expression of the catholic Church by rejecting the complicity of relativism and hegemonic monopoly.

IMAGININGS FOR A NEW ECUMENICAL APPEAL

Sometimes, I think that the deep reason for our brokenness could be the lack of authentic missionary commitment to witness to the catholicity of the gospel. Limitless relativism is possible only when we give up on human relationships with others. Isolationism or exclusive protectionism based on dogmatic principles are installed only when we give up on going beyond our own human boundaries. It could be the case that those who cannot open themselves to others hurt each other in the name of unity, catholicity, Scripture, and tradition.

As we see in 1 Peter 2:4-10, the Church is a priestly people of God, called to practice Christ's priesthood following his example. The

Christian Church is also the people and community for the justification, reconciliation, and sanctification of others. As Moberly said, the Church is "intense 'for-other-ness,'" that is, a people who live with the experiences of otherness.[10] Following Christ, the Church lives in unending calling to open itself to God and others. In this intense for-other-ness as an openness to others, Christians offer priestly sacrifice for reconciliation between God and others and between themselves and others. The Church is a fellowship and communion shaped by priestly sacrifice for reconciliation, that is, witness to the catholicity of God's love.

Kosuke Koyama argues convincingly that the gospel is essentially stranger-centered. An inclusive love for the "other" is at the heart of the biblical faith and is the defining characteristic of the early Church's understanding of the person and work of Christ.[11] Therefore, all churches and Christians must be constantly challenged, disturbed, and stirred up by the presence of strangers. However, not all the problems challenging and disturbing us are asking for a clear solution. The important thing is how we face and deal with the problems. Many problems we face in this earthly life are not susceptible of quick or perfect solution. Nonetheless, this impossibility need not lead to hopeless frustration and despair. Different outcomes, contrary to our expectations, are always possible.

A gift is not simply a thing that we decide will be a gift. To make something a gift, or to make a moment or situation the most blessed

---

10   R. C. Moberly, *Ministerial Priesthood* (London: John Murray, 1919), 256.

11   Kosuke Koyama, *Mount Fuji and Mount Sinai: A Pilgrimage in Theology* (London: SCM Press, 1984), 252.

time or space, is not simply about the thing, the moment, or the situation itself. *Relationship* transforms a thing into an irreplaceable gift. Likewise, what decides the outcome of a crisis, problem, or conflict, is not the crisis, problem, or conflict itself. It is the relationship around it that eventually decides the result. Therefore, how to face the crisis or problem, in what way and with whom, is decisive. The relationship that is formed among persons and with God around the problem can transform the problematic situation to become a journey toward the glory of resurrection. Without this belief, catholicity and *koinonia* or communion would not be possible. The profession of 1920 that "God wills fellowship" should be read as an invitation for us to participate relationships that may transform the situation of crisis and conflict.

A Korean writer who devoted his whole life to the democratization of society and spent more than 20 years in prison wrote:

> Seeking after truth is always accompanied by pains. Seeking after truth has no definite goal. Its goal is the summation of those pains. A trail path is different from a highway. A trail path, not a highway, leads us to the truth. The capitalist logic of the highway is ruled by speed and efficiency, while the humanist spirit of the trail path is filled with beauty and pleasure. We run along straight lines every day on highways. But an animal in the natural state never runs along straight lines, except when it has a predator behind it.[12]

---

12 "Seeking after Truth and Pains," Dobuleosup, available online; Shin Young Bock, *DamRon* (Seoul: Dolbege, 2015), 124.

On the way of seeking after truth, seemingly contradictory terms like pain, beauty, and pleasure meet together. These terms are reconciled into a radically transformed new relationship. Therefore, the summation of pain is also the summation of beauty and pleasure. The goal known to us through the summation of pain is provisional, not fixed. Reconciliation is not a goal that was already decided in the past. It is not the end of relationship. It is a journey without a goal, a journey endlessly moving beyond suggested goals. It is a journey in which walking together and sharing together is more important than the results. If we simply want to remove a problem, rather than achieve a deep reconciliation among peoples related by the problem, and if we want to stop at a point before the goal rather than go beyond all goals through the center of the path, we will choose the straight highway. But we will thereby become a predator or a prey.

I think there are four different human relationships. First is the relationship of dominance and subordination. It is like the relationship of lord and servant. The term *relationship* is not really proper here, because the connection is not truly human. It is the relationship of I and it, as Martin Buber said.[13] It can never challenge me or resist me. The second relationship is the relationship of contract, in which both sides are interdependent and interact in the expectation of mutual benefit. In many cases, the relationship is an alliance to keep their positions as predators and not to become prey. But the interdependent relationship is confined within the scope of the contract. Therefore, the relationship does not extend to issues outside of the established scope.

---

13 Martin Buber, *I and Thou*, trans. Walter Kaufmann (New York: Touchstone, 1996).

Third is a relationship in which people are devoted to a common cause. Because of the overwhelming weight of the common cause, there is not space for each person's peculiarity or difference in the relationship. The sacrifice for the greater goal becomes the totality of what each person has to achieve in her or his life. Although the goal is sacred, there is not an active relationship between the persons.

The last possible human relationship is the one in which the intensity of otherness is always alive. The relationship is an event by which we encounter others who can never be reduced to our own category of judgement and definition. It is an event in which I can see myself and my world from an absolutely transformed perspective known by the irreducible difference between us. This relationship is close to the fellowship or communion that our God wills. In this relationship, we have to open ourselves toward others, as we are invited by them. We will confess that it is possible only through Christ. We will feel the catholicity of God's love, fellowship, and communion.

Such catholicity is concretized by the Church's pursuit of truly living relationships in which openness to others and the intensity of otherness is alive. The pursuit of living relationships is revealed in biblical metaphors like a building built by living stones rather than dead ones, and a discipleship realized by friendship rather than the relationship of lord and servant. Such a pursuit of true living relationship with others amounts to a missionary commitment to witness to the catholicity of God's love and reveal the catholicity of the Church in the world. The statement on mission from the World Council of Churches, *Together Towards Life*, helpfully encourages a radical transformation of the mode of missionary interaction, "'from mission to the margins' to 'mission from the margins.'"[14] It is also a radical transformation of the way of witnessing to and revealing the catholicity of the Church.

It is time we followed this transformed way of witnessing to and revealing the catholicity of the Church. The crisis of our time is truly apocalyptic. The result of the crisis could be more tragic than any of the wars we have experienced in history. Very painfully, we may have to realize that the catastrophic end of life on earth is unavoidable. We don't know the way to stop the endless rush of marketization, commodification, and consumption. The cry of broken lives is no longer blocked by the rosy rhetoric of the market and technology worshipers. It is a time when an immediate and clear solution is needed.

Of course, we will not find a perfect solution. The rush toward catastrophe cannot be stopped in a moment. In this situation, we have to proclaim the gospel and the possibility of hope for our life on this earth. We cannot speak only of the remote future nor a new earth which is not yet contaminated. Catholicity based on such an understanding of space and time may not work anymore. Now, the wholeness of catholicity may have to be realized in the depth and density of a very short moment and a very limited space.

God's love *cannot* fail in such a moment and space of impossibility. God's love and God's fellowship will transform the most tragic moment to the most blessed moment through us, his faithful

---

14 World Council of Churches, "Together Toward Life: Mission and Evangelism in Changing Landscapes," in *Ecumenical Missiology: Changing Landscapes and New Conceptions of Mission*, ed. Kenneth R. Ross, Jooseop Keum, Kyriaki Avtzi and Roderick R. Hewitt (Oxford: Regnum, 2016), 357.

followers, and our ecclesial gathering. With this belief in the catholicity of God's love, we have to open ourselves and participate in the life of God's suffering people.

HUMBLE SUGGESTIONS FOR A NEW ECUMENICAL APPEAL

I will close with five programmatic suggestions for our collective consideration, both as Anglicans and ecumenically.

Signs of the Time

Christians are those who seek the *kairotic* meaning of time for their discipleship in this world. This is the meaning of time discerned in the relationship of God and the world. What they are seeking is time for God and for God's disciples. Thus, Christians are those who listen to God's calling amid contemporary crisis. As Greta Thunberg said, people are suffering. People are dying. Entire ecosystems are collapsing. We are at the beginning of a mass extinction. However, our political leaders are still talking only about money and fairy tales of eternal economic growth. In her challenging question *How dare you?* I see the crisis of old relationships, order, authority, and our understanding of catholicity and unity. In this crisis of our time, what are we called to be and to do? What is the will of God? What kind of fellowship and catholicity does God will? I hope to see all our ecumenical partners joining together to address this question of what time it is. In 1920, the bishops at the Lambeth Conference stated that they had gathered together "realising the responsibility which rests upon us at this time, and sensible of the sympathy and the prayers of many, both within and without our own Communion" (Appeal, intro.). In this time of crisis, I hope that not only the next Lambeth Conference but also future ecumenical gatherings can show the sincere attitude of seeking to discern the signs of the time, particularly in a situation where many political leaders still try to hide truth.

Catholicity and Fellowship as God Wills

The catholicity of the Church cannot be reduced only to the re-union, or even the fellowship, of divided churches. The scope of our understanding of catholicity, or of the catholic Church itself, should be expanded beyond the vision of ecclesial unity. To speak of *the catholic Church*, the catholicity of the Church, must mean that the Church has opened herself to God as the only one who can embrace the "mystery of the whole."[15] Likewise, it will mean that the Church has opened herself to others. The catholic Church is a Church living "other centered" mission, as Kosuke Koyama says.[16] It is a Church that can encounter unexpected others, and be constantly challenged, disturbed, and stirred up by the presence of strangers. We do not know the whole; only God knows the whole. For us the whole is an item of faith, given by God in Christ. *In* him, *in* the catholic love of God,

---

15 See Philip Sheldrake, "A Spirituality of Reconciliation: Encouragement for Anglicans from a Roman Catholic Perspective," *Journal of Anglican Studies* 6 (2008): 113.

16 Koyama, *Mount Fuji*, 252.

God himself and his catholic Church may be participated — beyond our present boundaries and accustomed, pre-theological securities. In order to live the catholicity and fellowship that God wills, we must travel beyond the bounds of our own understanding.

Openness and Vulnerability to Others

The Fifth World Conference on Faith and Order in Santiago de Compostela (1993) spoke of "daring to be open and vulnerable to each other."[17] Such openness (*kenosis*) and vulnerability (*metanoia*) should be expressed not only in the ecumenical fellowships of church families but also in our daring to encounter those whom we have made "other" in the present crisis. I hope that openness and vulnerability animate all Christian gatherings, including the next Lambeth Conference, as an embodiment of the proper catholicity of the Church. In this way, we may also witness to the truth over against the would-be coercive hegemony of too many nations and political leaders.

Crisis of Humanity

We have failed to reconcile humanity and nature. We live in a time where human beings and common natural resources alike are ruthlessly commodified and consumed. We don't know yet how humanity and scientific technologies can be reconciled and live together.

17 World Council of Churches, *Fifth World Conference on Faith and Order, Santiago de Compostela 1993: Message, Section Reports, Discussion Paper,* Faith and Order Paper No. 164 (Geneva: WCC Publications, 1993), 11.

Paradoxically, amid a great welter of technological knowing, we hear of the extinction of life on this planet. Our age is marked by a deep disappointment in humanity. In this time of crisis, we must say again who we are in relation to God and our neighbors, including in terms of nature and technology. We have many studies and statements on theological anthropology from ecumenical dialogues, but we need to encourage them to do more. The most important cause of contemporary crisis may be found in our perception of the human being.

Anglican Vocation for Fellowship and Catholicity

The Anglican way has been explained with concepts like *via media*, comprehensiveness, and dispersed authority as particular modes of synthesizing or "traditioning" experience and discovery.[18] Amid complicatedly entangled situations, Anglicans have often sought neither to exclude nor deny others in their assertions of confessional identity. We have sought to bear tensions and differences, rather than to achieve quick resolution. We have viewed conflicts as opportunities for new relationship and discovery rather than as reasons for antagonism. In this way, we have hoped to bear witness to God's own catholicity, as an embrace of the whole.

Archbishop Desmond Tutu often testified to his confidence in the universal desire for forgiveness and reconciliation in the human

---

18 On *traditioning*, see Walter Brueggemann and Tod Linafelt, *An Introduction to the Old Testament: The Canon and Christian Imagination* (Louisville: Westminster John Knox Press, 2012), 10-15.

mind and spirit.[19] Even when we are mired in conflict, we desire these things. That being so, our suffering presents an opportunity to renew the call to reconciliation, unity, and fellowship. Amid the present Anglican crisis, the catholic vocation stretches beyond our own Communion, summoning us to openness and vulnerability to *all* others. As we are stirred and challenged by them, we will see again how to move beyond division and conflict within our Communion and between church families.

19   Desmond Mpilo Tutu, *No Future Without Forgiveness* (New York: Doubleday, 2000), 116-118; "Foreword" in *Forgiveness and Reconciliation*, ed. Raymond G. Helmick, S.J., and Rodney L. Petersen (Pennsylvania: Templeton Foundation Press, 2001), ix-xiii.

NINE

Broader Ecology of Anglicanism

Hannah Matis

We have been asked to consider the Anglican call to unity today, and its potential appeal to the whole Church. Ephesians 4 entreats us to "bear with one another in love, making every effort to maintain the unity of the Spirit in the bond of peace," and I have taken that as my model and my ideal in what follows.

Ephesians, of course, goes on to describe the different functions of the various members of the body, in what Gregory the Great once called "unity in diversity."[1] While I acknowledge the gift of authority

---

1   R. A. Markus, *Gregory the Great and His World* (Cambridge: Cambridge University Press, 1997), 73: "Diversity in unity was the keynote of his conception of the Christian community. It became the guiding thread of the pastoral principles formulated in the *Regula Pastoralis*; and this it

granted to us in the historical episcopate, as a church historian and a specialist in the early Middle Ages in particular, I see diversity, even theological diversity, as the concrete reality of the Christian historical experience. The early Church developed in multiple urban centers simultaneously throughout the Roman Empire; the wholesale destruction of Jerusalem ensured, among other things, that there would be no one city that both claimed to be the single head of these various communities and could really make good on that claim. This regionalism is to some extent glossed over or concealed by modern western notions of what constitutes systematic theology. Any patristics scholar can tell you that even the great ecumenical councils of the Church are best understood as waystations along the road of ongoing Christian theological debate, rather than destinations wherein unity was fully achieved. In fact, councils such as Chalcedon were most destructive of Christian unity when their conclusions were imposed by fiat.[2] In the work both of reconciliation and of theological debate, an easy trap is

remained throughout his practice as bishop. The purpose of organisation and hierarchy in the church was to foster diversity within unity."

2   See Rowan Williams, *Arius: Heresy and Tradition* (London: Darton, Longman, and Todd, 1987); Lewis Ayres, *Nicaea and Its Legacy: An Approach to Fourth-Century Trinitarian Theology* (Oxford: Oxford University Press, 2004); *The Making of Orthodoxy: Essays in Honour of Henry Chadwick,* ed. Rowan Williams (Cambridge: Cambridge University Press, 2011); Khaled Anatolios, *Retrieving Nicaea: The Development and Meaning of Trinitarian Doctrine* (Grand Rapids: Baker Academic, 2011); *Chalcedon in Context: Church Councils 400-700*, ed. Richard Price and Mary Whitby (Liverpool: Liverpool University Press, 2009); Brian Daley, *God Visible: Patristic Christology Reconsidered* (Oxford: Oxford University Press, 2018); Peter Brown, *The Rise of Western Christendom: Triumph and Diversity*, 2nd edn. (Oxford: Wiley-Blackwell, 2003); Jack Tannous, *The*

to hustle participants toward a happy ending or easy resolution that they cannot yet feel or affirm. Unity cannot be achieved by forcing a theological settlement on people prematurely. I refer the British to their own history in this regard.

So, should we give up? By no means! But let us at least be realistic about the nature and scale of the problem. At Lambeth 2022 the bishops of the Anglican Communion will be dealing with an unprecedented level of cultural and theological diversity within and without the Church, of a sort their forebears of 1920 could not have imagined. At the same time, Lambeth in 1920 had experienced the heyday of the international missionary movement and met in the wake of the Great War. Lambeth 2022 will be meeting in a world in which nationalistic political rhetoric appears to be more attractive and effective than it has for several generations. For these reasons, among others, the Church in the West now possesses a local, provincial—in the negative sense of the word—understanding of its place within the Anglican Communion.

I see some of the effects and affects of this in my professional situation. The Episcopal Church has always been a minority denomination in America, and in many places mimics the congregationalist sea in which it swims. Add to that the ecumenical pattern of the contemporary Episcopal Church. Case in point: a majority of my students at Virginia Theological Seminary were not born into the Episcopal Church, and many are very new to the Anglican tradition. As a faculty we often feel that we spend three years educating our seminarians into a basic, introductory understanding of the church they have just

Making of the Medieval Middle East: Religion, Society, and Simple Believers (Princeton: Princeton University Press, 2018).

joined, rather than anything more advanced. In both the Church of England and in the Episcopal Church, many of our students are also significantly older—with a lifetime's experience in their local area, but little sense of the wider Anglican world. If we as teachers do our jobs well, we complicate somewhat our students' understanding of how to define "the church" or "their church," to make it greater than their local community, their local diocese, or their national church. A week ago, I was at a meeting of Virginia Theological Seminary's Center for Anglican Communion Studies, where without exception every student present begged for resources with which they could educate their local parishes that were, willfully or otherwise, clueless about the Anglican Communion and the Lambeth Conference. To be honest, I found this both depressing and hopeful.

❀ ❀ ❀

As the Anglican Communion heads into Lambeth 2022 and whatever will follow, I believe we are all called to explain, and even reinvent, our church as something *beyond* a gathering or a network of bishops and primates. Historically, the Church has of course always formulated its doctrine via gatherings of bishops, and such gatherings still potentially possesses great authority with which to do so. The Lambeth Conference has, however, never arrogated that authority to itself. To be sure, if it looks like a synod, and meets like a synod, and sounds like a synod, why doesn't it operate as one? On the other hand, if it were a synod, how would it connect the congregationalist parishes of Virginia, the English Home Counties, *and* Sydney's Western Suburbs?

If we are to have real communion, if real reconciliation between us is to take root, we need to teach a new generation of clergy and lay-people what the Communion is and why it matters. Given our recent acrimonious history, all of us need to explain how walking together is a positive good, even if something like a patient witness to brokenness is the best we can muster until a season for true growth arrives. *A bishop brings his diocese*, it was once said about the Lambeth Conference. How do bishops carry Lambeth home? And is it really just the *bishops'* responsibility? How does the Anglican Communion properly claim the consultative and communicative role allotted to the laity in the Anglican Consultative Council (ACC)? How might the laywoman bring her diocese to the ACC, and how can she bring the ACC home? As she does so, she will bring the Anglican Communion home as well, and thereby a part of the worldwide Church of Christ.

Lambeth 1920 suggested that the Anglican Communion should be a microcosm of the Church's engagement with the world, as the cataclysmic effects of World War I drew the bishops together in repentance. With this as a guiding principle, many forces will, or should, draw us together again, across our many differences. Pragmatic, ecumenical practicums in the substance of *walking together* will, I believe, be essential, not least to show the world why the Anglican Communion matters. Here, I would highlight four forces that should inspire a united Anglican response.

Now and in the coming decades, climate change will affect all human beings, most notably in the Global South. But the greatest share of responsibility, and indeed repentance, must be borne by the North. For many of our brothers and sisters, drought, water shortages, harvest failure, storm damage, flooding, and rising sea levels, all of which we place under the umbrella of "climate change," are the inescapable issue of our day. And when might it become the apocalypse of our day? The fifth Anglican mark of mission is to strive to safeguard the integrity of creation and sustain and renew the life of the earth. Up to now this has been hazy and largely aspirational. As western society comes under pressure to change its habits, even radically, for the next generation, climate change presents a pastoral problem in need of address. Can we congratulate ourselves for recycling peanut butter jars and buying Tesla pickup trucks? An honest reckoning with the problem can also help replace the provincial and isolationist attitudes of both past and present with something more concertedly international and interconnected. Likewise, in the Global South, a green energy revolution could transform society in many unexpected ways, which in turn will challenge how the Church can support its people. This necessarily would open new opportunities for communication, mission, and pastoral care in remote areas.

A second, related force for change and potential unity among us is the plight of the refugee and the immigrant, whose numbers, we are told, will only increase in coming decades. The face of the Anglican Communion in the Episcopal Church *is,* overwhelmingly, the refugee and the immigrant. Our lone seminarian at VTS from the diocese of Nebraska—a historically very white, rural, agricultural part of Midwestern America—is a Dinka from South Sudan. The Sudanese refugee community, however, has maintained an ambivalent relationship, at best, with the Episcopal Church. Refugees and immigrants in our churches can potentially serve as cultural ambassadors between our different contexts. Both the Global South and the Global North should unite in their support.

The third force for change and potential unity is the experience of contemporary Christian martyrs. Christians are often the poor and dispossessed right now, including Anglican Christians, notwithstanding, and in some cases because of, our privileged imperial past. Let all Christians, and all Anglicans, tell the stories of the martyrs, grieve and rejoice together without vengeance, honor one another in the story-telling, and draw near in their sacrifice, remembering that the Son of Man had no place to lay his head.

The fourth force for change and potential unity is the teaching of our own Anglican tradition. There *is* an Anglican tradition of scholarship and teaching, and it is a tradition worth preserving. We almost lost Notre Dame Cathedral several years ago, through a sincere, but clumsy, desire to renovate. It required supreme courage from the firefighters of Paris for us to prize again what almost slipped away. Are we in danger of losing the good—as well as the bad, contradictory, and ambiguous—treasures of our tradition through similar neglect or misplaced desires to innovate? If we do not develop new educational structures by which to transmit and explain the faith, we will lose it. Certainly we will lose its range, depth, and complexity. To make an analogy with ecology, if we do not create the theological equivalent of a seed bank, what will survive will be multiple, disparate, vulnerable regional monocultures. From the standpoint of someone who designs and plans seminary curricula, I find myself constantly wanting to use more voices from around the Communion in my classes, and not always knowing where to begin. Wouldn't it be wonderful if we had a body of Anglican theology—Anglican theologians, lay and ordained—writing in their local languages, with facing-page English translation?

※ ※ ※

In the face of these serious challenges facing us, may I sound a note of calm? In his recent book on Christology, Rowan Williams notes, in a discussion on Dietrich Bonhoeffer and Eric Przywara, that both "see the primary Christian calling in the modern age as a recovery of apostolic reticence—not a nervous self-consciousness about professing faith in public but in a sense the exact opposite, a confidence that God's active indwelling does not need to be insisted upon either with exaggerated aesthetic gestures or with anxious political aggressiveness." God's indwelling does does not require grand gesture because, as Williams goes on to say, "Christian ethics is not about dramatic and solitary choices for individual good or evil but the steady building of a culture of durable mutuality and compassion." In the world created and saved by Christ, we see God's grace most clearly as "durable, attentive love."[3]

Durable mutuality and compassion. Durable, attentive love. What is fellowship, what is communion, what is Christian witness pointing toward Christian unity, if not these?

---

3 Rowan Williams, *Christ: The Heart of Creation* (London: Bloomsbury Continuum, 2018), 245, 247.

PART III

Reflections on Ministry and Practice

✳ ✳ ✳

TEN

Repentance and the Role of Bishops

Jenny Andison

I felt honoured to join Dr. Jane Williams, Bishop Christopher Cocksworth, and Bishop Joseph Wandera for the closing panel of our colloquium at Lambeth Palace, to reflect together on key themes and questions that emerged from our conversations, and to connect them to my own context. At the time, I was serving as Area Bishop in the York-Credit Valley within the Diocese of Toronto. I now serve as rector of St. Paul's, Bloor Street, in the same wonderful diocese. The two themes that emerged for me with urgency, as aspects of the ecumenical vocation of Anglicans, were repentance and the role of bishops in the Church—and, yes, the two are connected!

REPENTANCE

This oft despised or misunderstood word was a central and fruitful theme in our time together and should be retrieved. In our session on the vocation of Anglicanism 100 years on from the 1920 Lambeth Conference, Professor Charlotte Methuen demonstrated that, from the first drafts, the "Appeal to all Christian People" contained a clear acknowledgement that our Christian unity is obscured through the sinfulness and failings of Christians. We are our own stumbling block.[1] To the degree that the Anglican Communion sees itself as part of the one, holy, catholic, and apostolic Church, we must acknowledge that our sinfulness as a Communion has contributed to the disunity of the Church and the obscuring of the witness of the Church to the nations of the world. What does this mean in our own local contexts? How are individual dioceses obscuring the deep unity of the Church that exists in Christ Jesus? Where are dioceses being called corporately to repent of actions that have contributed to disunity in the Body of Christ? These are challenging questions that defy simplistic or clear-cut answers. But awkward, searching questions still need to be asked.

Ephraim Radner views repentance as the "ethical motor" of the Anglican Communion, without which we may increasingly struggle to find a rationale for life together.[2] Only an ethic of repentance will put the Anglican Communion on the right side of history. Only an

---

1   For a revised version of Charlotte Methuen's presentation, see chapter 1, above.

2   For a revised version of Ephraim Radner's presentation, see chapter 5, above.

ethic of repentance will enable the divisions to be healed and open the way for the Communion fully to enjoy the gift of Christ's unity again.

If this is true, what next steps shall we take as the Anglican Communion? First of all, each and every one of us should resolve to come afresh to our Lord in repentance—for all our many sins and offences, and most especially for those that have led to greater disunity in the Body. We also should grieve and lament, both publicly and privately, the disunity within our own ecclesial family. This disunity makes it challenging, but not impossible, for us to engage ecumenically in the healing of ecclesial wounds in the wider Church of Christ.

I can attest that the marvelous diversity and sad divisions in the wider Anglican Communion are mirrored in the Diocese of Toronto, including in the Area of the York-Credit Valley.[3] The Area comprises 50 different parishes and ministries, among which, on any given Sunday, in addition to English, services are being conducted, entirely or in part, in Cantonese, Mandarin, Punjabi, Malayalam, Spanish, Italian, and Portuguese. There are also Mongolian, Sudanese, Kenyan, Igbo, and Ghanaian congregations. As the parishes of York-Credit Valley join in the Anglican Cycle of prayer each Sunday, they are less inclined to lament their broken relationships and the disputes that bring disunity. And yet, they—we all—should. In the Area and within the broader Diocese of Toronto, we suffer divisions that ought rightly to be lamented and renounced. There is a greater unity to be sought,

---

3   The Episcopal Area of York-Credit Valley covers the western half of the City of Toronto, the City of Mississauga, and the rapidly expanding Region of Peel, which includes the City of Brampton and the greater Brampton area.

and healing that needs to take place—not only on the issues of the day, such as the question of same-gender marriage, but regarding how we are to move forward as a church in our post-Christian culture.

In the same spirit of repentance, we have an opportunity to be led into greater times of prayer, both within the diocese and ecumenically across the city of Toronto. As a microcosm of our world, I can't think of a better place than Greater Toronto for Christians of all denominations to come together in prayerful repentance, that our divisions may be healed for the sake of God's mission to the world.

THE ROLE OF BISHOPS

Reflecting on the fourth point of the Chicago-Lambeth Quadrilateral, the historic episcopate locally adapted, Dr. Methuen asked the wonderful question, "How adaptive can episcopacy really be?" given that it is such a sticking point in our ecumenical relationships. The historic episcopate was named as a challenge in the "Appeal" back in 1920, and it continues as an ecumenical challenge—for the same reasons (as demonstrated in the papers by Jeremy Worthen, Jamie Hawkey, and Christopher Cocksworth), and due to the consecration of women to the episcopate in many parts of the Anglican Communion. Meanwhile, as Professor Michael Root reminded us in his examination of the Anglican–Roman Catholic dialogue in the century since the 1920 Lambeth, Anglicans need to continue to wrestle with the Catholic Church's understanding of the Bishop of Rome's ability to speak infallibly.[4] On all counts, bishops can be stumbling blocks (*cue rueful laughter*), and we are right to ask, as we approach and continue beyond Lambeth 2022: where we can go from here with regard to episcopacy?

The Lambeth Conference presents a marvelous opportunity for bishops to explore and perhaps embrace Radner's summons to a sense of "corporate asceticism." What would we be willing to lay down sacrificially, or restrain ourselves from, to protect the integrity of the Communion as we deepen our life together? How might we slow down decision making on contentious issues in our dioceses that impact the wider Communion, in order to repair our frayed bonds of collegiality?

If we can embrace corporate asceticism at Lambeth 2022 and beyond, a happy byproduct may be that time and space are created for three other opportunities to emerge: to play together, pray together, and speak together. Bishops have the opportunity to build friendships ecumenically at the local level: to break bread with one another and share joys and challenges. These friendships can lead to partnership in adventure and mission. Consider what missional endeavors we could sponsor with our episcopal colleagues from other traditions. Consider also what may be achieved—and what has always been achieved—when we pray together.

I wonder if God is not deliberately driving us to our knees together in prayer, across ecumenical lines, just as so much power, status, and authority is being stripped away from the Western church. The Spirit of God may be calling us into deeper times of ecumenical play and prayer as bishops in our cities. Such times of prayer together may

---

4   For a revised version of Michael Root's presentation, see chapter 4, above.

in turn lead us to speak *together* as bishops across denominations on issues of great importance, like David Sheppard and Derek Worlock in Liverpool in the 1980s, and like so many others.[5] Pope Francis makes the front pages on a regular basis, often with reference to his ecumenical friends. His example can urge us to speak with a united voice as often as we can. Flowing out of prayer and an increasing sense of joint mission and gospel adventure, let us speak episcopally together on the issues of the day. Let's speak about our relationships with our Indigenous sisters and brothers, climate damage, migrants, homelessness, the increase in gun-related violence; and about the need to draw closer together in faith and order, in God's good time.

In addition to repenting together and lamenting together, bishops should go on playful mission together, pray together, and speak with one voice together, whenever and wherever the Lord will graciously permit.

FINAL QUESTIONS

I went home from our colloquium pondering two questions. Recognizing that answers will not be easy or clear-cut, I pray these questions may be a gift to you as they were to me.

First, what method or approach will we adopt for this next season of what Dr. Root calls "the normal phase of ecumenism"? And how shall we accommodate or adjust to the increasingly post-denominational

---

5 See, among others, Sheppard and Worlock, *Better Together: Christian Partnership in a Hurt City* (London: Darton, Longman and Todd, 2013).

posture of the younger generation in our Western, secular context?

When I was in parish ministry in the late 1990s and 2000s, I became increasingly aware that younger people who were looking for a church were rarely looking for an Anglican church; they just wanted a "good church." In 2018, I was able to attend the third Gathering of the Global Christian Forum (GCF) in Bogotá, Colombia, on behalf of the Anglican Communion and was intrigued by their simple ecumenical methodology. The GCF urges the telling of personal faith stories between Christians of varying denominations and emphasizes the building of relationships of trust in the field. This simple methodology is bearing fruit between different Protestant churches, to start; it will be interesting to see if it bears still wider fruit.

This method may also be the way forward locally as we Canadian Anglicans engage with young and vigorous evangelical denominations. These denominations are not necessarily asking the same questions that are debated in traditional ecumenical dialogues—concerning the historic episcopate, for example—and so the sharing of personal faith stories may be a good starting point for such new conversations.

Such local story sharing can also be a jumping-off point for the sharing of resources for mission. Historic denominations could conceivably share their valuable real estate assets, which are often under-utilized, with new and young church plants. The wisdom and experience of the historic denominations could support, guide, and enrich these church plants. Such fresh partnerships may, in turn, bear fruit in ecumenical conversations.

Second, what particular charism is the Anglican Communion hoping to bring to ecumenical conversations in the future? Dr. Radner mused that the age of a special Anglican charism within ecumenical conversations may in fact be over. *Not so fast*, I thought. We would do well to ask ourselves if we still can offer a *via media* within the wider Christian family. Experientially I would say *yes*, because Anglicans are seeking to hold together all these theological strains and tensions— catholic, charismatic, evangelical—within our own common life. If our internal struggles lead us into greater prayer and repentance, these may open surprising and exciting new conversations with young, growing, free churches, while we ourselves perhaps wait a while longer in a kind of stasis. As Western societies, at least, suffer more and more from polarization, both politically and economically, the *via media* may be a gift that Anglicans can again offer to a fractured world and Church. If and as we manage, by God's grace, to heal something of our own divisions in the Anglican family, the *via media* may have something visible and appreciable with which to commend itself.

I distinctly remember my first six months of episcopal ministry. I spent more time in repentance in my prayer life than at any other time, mainly repenting of all the terrible things I had ever thought of bishops! Repentance is a necessary step along the path toward renewal—in parishes, dioceses, and across the Anglican Communion. May God bless us in our ecumenical vocation as Anglicans, as we walk toward Lambeth 2022, and the future that our Heavenly Father is preparing for us. The whole of our ecclesial lives is only ever possible because God wills fellowship.

ELEVEN

Church as Bridge Builder in the World

Christopher Cocksworth

"We, Archbishops of the Holy Catholic Church... assembled from divers parts of the earth... under the presidency of the Archbishop of Canterbury... within two years of the ending of the Great War, give you greeting in the name of our Lord and Saviour, Jesus Christ."[1] So begins the encyclical letter of the 1920 Lambeth Conference. Confident of the *catholicity* of their churches, conscious of their *oneness* from across the nations, convinced that the guidance of the Spirit in the particular "conditions of the time" had laid upon them

---

1   Lambeth Conference 1920, "Encyclical Letter to the Faithful in Jesus Christ," in *The Lambeth Conferences, 1867–1930: The Reports of the 1920 and 1930 Conferences, with Selected Resolutions from the Conferences of 1867, 1878, 1888, 1897, and 1908* (London: SPCK, 1948), 23.

244 Christopher Cocksworth

an urgent *apostolic* mission, the bishops of the Anglican Communion presented to the world and the Church a compelling vision of *holiness*.[2] To a world "full of trouble and perplexity,"[3] torn apart by the catastrophic events of the First World War, the bishops proclaimed that the way to peace is through fellowship. To a divided church, where fellowship had been broken, the bishops appealed for reunion, "not as a laudable ambition or a beautiful dream, but as an imperative necessity," without which the Church's mission "in these times of peril" would be fatally wounded.[4]

"God wills fellowship," they declared, because "by God's own act" fellowship had been established through Jesus Christ (Appeal, §I). Fellowship, they said, is the "one idea" that "runs through all our work." They implored the Church to rise to the calling of the hour by recognising the world's cry for mutuality and by working with every manifestation of human fellowship in order "to deepen and purify it, and, above all, to attach it to God." To do so effectively, "the Church must itself be a pattern of fellowship." Only then will it be able to "win the world for fellowship."[5]

Every bishop ordained into the Church of God is situated in the world God made and redeemed. The interconnection between the Church and the world is dramatically set before my eyes every time I preach and preside in my cathedral. In place of a wall of stone at the

---

3   *Ibid.*, 33.

4   *Ibid.*, 24; Lambeth Conference 1920, "Resolutions Formally Adopted by the Conference," in *Lambeth Conferences*, 37.

5   "Encyclical Letter," 23–24.

west end, Coventry has a great screen of glass. Beyond the faces of the faithful gathered for worship, and through the images of saints and angels etched onto the glass, I look out onto the world. I see the ruins of the old cathedral destroyed in war during a fateful night in 1940 and my eyes are confronted with a world of "fear and despair," as the bishops put it in 1920 after another war had damaged the fabric of human life.[6] As I look over the ruined walls that still stand after all these years, calling to mind the fragility of civilisation, I see the City Council House and my thoughts turn to local politicians and officials seeking to shape Coventry's common life and the activities that sustain it. As my eyes return to a closer distance, I see passers-by pause, look one way to the ruins of the old, then the other way to the splendour of the new, and I imagine them wondering whether the Church can help them make sense of their lives in the world caught between despair and hope, pain and beauty.

In one corner of Coventry Cathedral there is another distinctive feature of its architecture. It is a chapel, conical in shape, like a wigwam, with a floor that draws everything to the centre. Although part of the cathedral structure, it is beyond the bishop's jurisdiction. This is the Chapel of Unity that belongs to all the churches. It was built with the same Christian instinct that inspired the bishops in 1920 to connect the healing of the nations with a mandate for the unity of the churches.

The energy of Lambeth 1920's encyclical letter and its ambitious "Appeal to All Christian People" derives from the capacity of these texts to speak simultaneously to the Church *and* to the world,

6   *Ibid.*, 33.

since the Church's priestly vocation entails hope for all humanity. At Lambeth Conference 2022, bishops will arrive again from "divers parts of the earth," from particular contexts and callings to serve a singular world for which Christ died.[7] What word of hope will they have for the peoples of the world today? How can their words serve the Word of the gospel that lifts the life of the world into the purposes of God?

❋ ❋ ❋

Our colloquium of October 2019 in Lambeth Palace—where the bishops of the Anglican Communion had gathered in 1920, from which place the Lambeth Conference takes its name—convened during a period of deep national trauma for the United Kingdom. Our Parliament, like the country it represents, was polarised and the machinery of government was grinding to a halt. The question of the UK's departure from the European Union was still not resolved and divisions in the country between "Brexiteers" and "Remainers," close to a 50-50 split, were playing out in Parliament, almost to the point of constitutional crisis. The week before the colloquium, the Supreme Court of the land had deemed the Prime Minister's decision to prorogue—suspend—Parliament to be unlawful, and declared it null and of no effect.

The court hearing was complicated, involving two simultaneous cases. It promised to include both finely tuned legal arguments and serious constitutional judgments. It did not disappoint. Aidan O'Neill,

---

7   *Ibid.,* 23.

representing Joanna Cherry against the government, referred to the arrangements of buildings around the Supreme Court as "an iconography of the state"—taking in not only the Houses of Parliament, opposite, but also

> across the square, Parliament; to the right, Westminster Abbey, the church; to the left, buildings of government. Four pillars of the state. Parliament to legislate, Church to pontificate, ...government to regulate, judges to adjudicate.[8]

To the untrained ear it could have sounded as if the barrister were dismissing the Church as irrelevant to the great issues of the day. While others make key decisions and exercise real power, the Church endlessly talks. But Aidan O'Neill's mind is highly trained in ancient languages as well as constitutional law. Drawing on the Latin derivation of *pontificate* as the making of bridges, he was acknowledging a fundamental place for the work of the Church in contemporary society. Law needs to be created, applied, and upheld. But people need more than law. They need the grace to understand each other and to live well together. They need the gospel. O'Neill's constitutional contention has been borne out in the UK as a number of bodies—both individuals and institutions—have invited the Archbishop of Canterbury to play a lead part in a project of national reconciliation. Bishops in their own dioceses have found similar roles more locally. A

---

8   Aidan O'Neill, quoted in Dulcie Lee, Claire Heald, and Francesca Gillett, "Supreme Court hears arguments over prorogation," *BBC* (18 Sept. 2019), available online.

Muslim councillor in Coventry City Council said to me: "Bishop, we need your help. We are all so divided. Only the Church can bring us together again."

The UK facing up to leaving the EU is, of course, very particular to one time and one place. Moreover, the Church of England rather unusually retains a constitutional role in the nation. The urgent need for bridging divides between people, communities, and nations, however, is both universal and perennial. The German sociologist, Hartmut Rosa, contends that alienation in relationships on all levels is a chief ill of the modern world. It is so pervasive that it has produced an alienation from the world itself. All relations suffer muteness, deadening.[9]

Rosa commends a rediscovery of "resonant space" where "two entities in relation... mutually affect each other in such a way that they can be understood as *responding to each other, ... each speaking with its own voice.*"[10] Rosa contrasts this with an echo, in which we hear our own voice reflected back to us. Resonance is different. The other voice is always other, always in some sense unavailable; but, truly spoken and truly heard, a connection is created—or, perhaps, restored. The possibility of new relationship appears.

Rosa does not write as a Christian, as far as I know. He makes no explicit reference to a theological framework. His categories, though, are deeply theological and ecclesial. The Church is founded on the restoration of resonance between God and the world, a restoration

---

9   See Hartmut Rosa, *Resonance*, trans. James C. Wagner (Cambridge: Polity Press, 2016).

10   Rosa, *Resonance*, 166–67; italics in original.

more radical than Rosa envisages. Although humanity is always different from God and never subsumed, God *assumes* humanity in Jesus Christ so fully that the Word is made flesh and spoken among us. Human words are uttered by God. The letter to the Colossians puts it succinctly: "in him the fullness of God was pleased to dwell, and through him God was pleased to reconcile all things to himself, whether on earth or in heaven, by making peace through the blood of the cross" (Col. 1:19-20).

The restoration of resonance between God and the world implies the restoration of relationships between the peoples of the world, who may be "clothed with the new self." As St. Paul continues: "In that renewal there is no longer Greek and Jew, circumscribed and uncircumscribed, barbarian, Scythian, slave and free; but Christ is all in all" (Col. 3:10-11). The Church, as Paul contends in his second letter to the Corinthians, is entrusted with the message and ministry of reconciliation. It entreats the people of the world to be reconciled with God and, in so doing, to reconcile with each other (2 Cor. 5:18-21).

Just here we meet the same conundrum faced by the bishops of Lambeth 1920. We cannot win the world for fellowship unless we embody authentic fellowship—resonant relationship—within our own life as the Church, *in* Jesus Christ in whom "all things hold together" (Col. 1:17). Now as then, mission to the world requires unity in the Church. As Jeremy Worthen writes succinctly in the present volume: "Communication of the gospel and communion of the churches are inseparable."[11]

---

11 Worthen, chapter 3, above. Cf. Worthen's outworking of the principle in "The Centenary of the 'Appeal to All Christian People' and the

※ ※ ※

The Appeal to all Christian People was a bold, some would say auda-
cious, attempt at bridge building. The bishops reached out to epis-
copally- and non-episcopally ordered churches alike, holding out
a vision of a re-united Church in which the many gifts of presently
divided Christians would be held in common. The bishops surely
sought to live out the historical self-identification of Anglicanism as a
meeting point between Catholics and Protestants. They also drew on
the categories of the Spirit, in a way that anticipated some of the no-
table ecclesial developments (the rise of Pentecostalism) and theological interests (pneumatology) of the coming 20th century. Fellowship
is the work of the Holy Spirit; it is the life of God that the Spirit
brings. Their emphasis on the Spirit led them to call the churches "to
try a new approach to reunion; to adopt a new point of view; to look
up to the reality as it is in God," and so accept that unity is constituted by God and may be found in an already existing "fellowship
in the Spirit."[12] Their pneumatological categories helped them express
the commonality of Christian people and their particularity in the
purposes of God. As they wrote: "It is not by reducing the difference
of Christians to uniformity, but by rightly using their diversity, that
the Church can become all things to all men. So long as there is vital

---

Ecumenical Vocation of Anglicanism," *Theology*, 123/2 (March-April
2020), 104-112.

12 "Encyclical Letter," 24-27.

connexion with the Head, there is positive value in the differentiation of the members."[13]

One hundred years on from the Appeal, the Church remains divided and disappointments abound. Nevertheless, there have been remarkable steps forward in the restoration of relationships—in some places great and brave leaps, leading to organic union between churches, including Anglican churches. Despite challenges to our own unity, Anglicans are still called by God to bridge divides between episcopal and non-episcopal churches.

One such responsibility is to find "a new approach to reunion; to adopt a new point of view" on the ministry of the Bishop of Rome.[14] The Anglican and Roman communions remain a long way from the sort of full communion that many in the 20th century thought entirely possible. Nevertheless, a respect for the office of the Bishop of Rome has grown that is worthy of formal acknowledgement. In a world that has become self-evidently global, the role of a global minister embodied in the pope makes sense in a new sort of way. The prophetic ministry of John Paul II, the teaching ministry of Benedict XVI, and the missional ministry of Francis, *all* world-wide in their reach, have done much to convince non-Roman Catholics of the value of a universal Petrine ministry. The time is ripe for an expression of respect for the office of the pope that, notwithstanding remaining differences and disagreements, seeks a relationship with genuine institutional characteristics that may advance the incipient reconciliation of our churches.[15]

---

13   *Ibid.*, 25.

14   *Ibid.*, 25.

15   See more fully the conclusion to ARCIC II's *Gift of Authority* (1998), §60.

Another *new approach to reunion* could propose imaginative ways in which the problematic side of Lambeth 1920 might be overcome. On the one hand, the bishops affirmed that the ministries of those ordained in non-episcopally ordered churches are "manifestly blessed and owned by the Holy Spirit as effective means of grace" (Appeal, §VII). On the other, the bishops denied those same ministers a sacramental ministry until they receive episcopal ordination, even when the sort of union under the sign of episcopacy envisaged by the Appeal is being effected. Some Anglican churches have managed to navigate this ecumenical maze, but flat-footed episcopal mandates still impede ecumenical progress toward unity in many places, including the Church of England.

Cannot a new point of view be found that both invites other churches to embrace episcopacy and allows Anglican bishops to embrace the ministries of those ordained within the ambit of another oversight (*episcopé*)? I believe that more of the Spirit's wisdom may be mined from the Appeal's own deployment of *commission*. The embrace of ministers into the apostolic mission led by the bishop rests at the heart of that which catholic order seeks to defend. It is objected that anything short of full-scale ordination (of course, *re*-ordination is foresworn as grave sin) falls short of our principles, and accordingly could undermine the very relations with Rome we rightly must consolidate, as I already suggested. My answer is that as inter-episcopal relations with Rome improve, we will be able to work more readily with Rome on a commonly acceptable solution.

※ ※ ※

Lambeth 1920 recognised that work toward inter-church unity needs to be supported by renewed activity that serves intra-church unity by improving and strengthening "in every way the fellowship of our own Church."[16] It will take more than the conclusion of this short piece to address the deep fissures in contemporary Anglicanism that will be all too evident in the 2022 Conference through the absence of bishops who have chosen to reject the Archbishop of Canterbury's invitation to convene and confer together in one communion. Stresses and strains within the Anglican Communion are not new, of course, and it is helpful to be reminded that the increasingly international character of the Communion faced the bishops of 1920 with their own problems. "The fact that the Anglican Communion has become world-wide forces upon it some of the problems which must always beset the unity of the Catholic Church itself."[17] The broader the catholicity, the greater the challenge to communion. The greater the challenge to communion, the deeper the gift of catholicity is to the world.

Today the diverse cultures of global humanity live in proximity to each other. The clash of world cultures (Chinese, Middle Eastern, European, African, North American, for example) and the clash of cultures within countries (seen starkly in the UK through our recent traumas) pose a real threat to the peace and prosperity of the world. Because the gospel is for all people in every place, the Church necessarily reaches across every culture, binding those different human cultures together in the life of Christ in whom "all things hold together" (Col. 1:17). In our diverse cultures, we learn how to live in

16   "Encyclical Letter," 26.

17   *Ibid.*

Christ amidst the realities of life in the world through our common scriptures, which tell of Christ and lead us, by the Spirit, to him. Like many, I found most valuable in the first Lambeth Conference I attended in 2008 the experience of listening to bishops from across the world engage with Scripture. Lambeth 2022 will be enlivened by a series of videos of people across the communion answering questions on 1 Peter, the main text of the Conference, such as:

"What does holy living look like?"
"Who are the exiles, strangers, or aliens in your part of the world?"
"What does it mean to be suffering for Christ?"
"How do you understand a shepherd in your culture?"
"Who are the 'roaring lions' that prowl about in your world?"

Bishops assembling and conferring from "diverse parts of the earth"[18] offer a remarkable opportunity for the Communion to illustrate to the world how different cultures can better understand each other through attentive listening. The Lambeth Conference has the capacity also to equip the Church to be better used by God as an instrument of reconciling love in the world.

I am conscious that my claims for the bridging capacity of Anglicanism could be seen to be susceptible to the sort of critique laid out by Michael Root in his paper.[19] I hope that they do not fall into the sort of presumptions that he fairly criticises, and I recognise that

18 *Ibid.*, 23.

19 For a revised version of Michael Root's presentation, see chapter 4, above.

the present momentum in the churches makes any sort of bridging between them more difficult. My argument, though, begins with the mission of the Church of Christ as a whole: the calling of the Body of Christ to a bridging ministry in the world. Entrusted with the gospel of reconciliation, we are to pontificate in the original sense of the word. We are to make bridges between people and to open their hearts and minds to the bridge between heaven and earth, God and humanity, that has been laid out for the world in the Incarnation, crucifixion, resurrection, and ascension of Jesus Christ, and the Pentecostal outpouring of the Holy Spirit on all flesh. The capacity to minister this gospel of reconciliation to the world is in direct proportion to the Church living out that gospel in its own life. My contention is that Anglicanism, despite its internal tensions—or rather, because of them—remains well placed to reach out to the whole Church: to become a fuller sign of the reconciled humanity that God purposes through Christ, and to serve as a more effectual means of its realisation, empowered by the Spirit of Fellowship.

TWELVE

Fellowship in God and the East African Revival

Joseph Wandera

Let us consider how to provoke one another to love and good deeds, not neglecting to meet together, as is the habit of some, but encouraging one another, and all the more as you see the Day approaching.

—HEB. 10:24-25

Gathered around the same space where Lambeth 1920 took place, all the speakers at the colloquium, drawn from different parts of the world, affirmed in varied ways the timeliness of Lambeth 1920: "God wills fellowship." The fact that we could meet to listen to each other in a context of love and respect is a miniature of the fellowship to which Lambeth 1920—and indeed the Anglican Communion today—invites us. By meeting, we form abiding friendships with brothers and sisters from around the world.

Professor Radner invites us to consider a "thick" approach to our understanding of this invitation to fellowship, one that goes beyond our present circumstances and is rooted in the very nature of Christ himself, whose fellowship with God and with us is utterly comprehensive (see chapter 5, above). In reflecting on Lambeth 1920, therefore, my starting point is to locate the call in my personal journey as a Christian, an Anglican, and a bishop, called to serve the Church in Kenya at a time when there is considerable longing for mutuality. At present, this work is framed for us under the Building Bridges Initiative (BBI) of President Uhuru Kenyatta and Opposition leader Raila Odinga. It was started in 2018 after President Kenyatta and his closest competitor in the 2017 presidential election, Odinga, decided to shake hands (now commonly referred to as *the handshake*) and unite the country that was at the brink of war. The initiative has ushered in a national discussion on the future of Kenya, with the aim of stemming the incessant ethnic and political tension and violence in the country. The call to fellowship certainly resonates in our context, and even more at the church level, on evangelical grounds. To speak of building bridges is to acknowledge that it will not be an event but a process, which calls for prayer, patience, and self-reflection.

I am a product of the work of the Church Missionary Society (CMS), which God sent to introduce the Anglican church in Kenya. Dr. Johann Ludwig Kraft, a Lutheran from Germany, working with CMS, arrived at the Palace of the Sultan of Zanzibar in 1844 and moved to Mombasa "to convert the unbelieving world."[1] The CMS heritage is an abiding part of my identity as an Anglican Christian. No wonder that up the present day my mother still refers to the Anglican Church as "CMS." To affirm our indebtedness to the early missionary work of CMS is also to affirm our heritage as part of the global Christian family. This heritage invites us to maintain continually an outlook on mission that is both global and local.

As a young boy growing up in my village's Anglican parish, I knew that the Anglican church was more than just myself in my own little place. I remember with nostalgia the visit to the Diocese of Mumias on 14 December 1994 by the then Archbishop of Canterbury, George Carey. The Church of the Province of Kenya, as it was called then, was celebrating one hundred years since the introduction of Anglicanism in Kenya by the CMS. We spent most of the day under the scorching tropical sun waiting for the archbishop. We had spent many days preparing to receive him. In him we saw and could connect with the global Anglican network. When he arrived, the level of joy and hospitality accorded by Anglicans in Mumias was immense. We were so happy and proud that he could find time to visit us and express solidarity with our then Diocesan Bishop William Wesa and the Christian community at large.

---

1 John Baur, *2000 Years of Christianity in Africa: An African History 62–1992*, 2nd edn. (Nairobi, Kenya: Pauline Publications Africa, 1998), 224.

In the Kenyan context, this sense of interconnectedness to the wider Anglican family is profound. It provides fertile ground for strengthening fellowship, including amid our common challenges. Archbishop Justin Welby, following in the footsteps of his predecessors, has similarly invested significant resources in visiting various provinces of our Anglican family to affirm and encourage our common bond. Such visits leave indelible footprints on the landscape of our common life.

Add to this the heritage of the East African Revival movement, which traces its origins to missionaries who came to us from the CMS in close partnership with indigenous African Christians. A medical missionary named John Edward ("Joe") Church was based in Rwanda from the late 1920s until the 1960s. Dr. Church played an important role in the East African Revival Movement, the origins of which were in 1933 at CMS's Gahini Hospital in Rwanda.[2] Upon serving for two years at Gahini Hospital, Church experienced a state of spiritual dryness. The broader context was that there had been a damaging famine in Rwanda and the personal circumstances of Dr. Church necessitated that he take leave in Uganda in 1929. There he encountered Simon Nsibambi, an African Christian, while staying at Namirembe, which meeting became the turning point of his spiritual journey and missionary work. Simon Nsibambi and Dr. Church discovered they were both concerned about the declining spiritual state of the Anglican Church in Uganda and consequently decided to spend the next two

---

2   Here and in the following paragraph, I depend upon the short biography of Church on the Boston University "History of Missiology" webpage, at www.bu.edu.

days in prayer and reading of the Bible. Their encounter represented a meeting point of two people from different cultures, both deeply concerned about the condition of the Church, and devoted to a spirituality of renewal.[3]

This movement was interdenominational and played an important role in spiritual revitalization in the 20th century. Although the revival emerged in the Anglican Church through a collaboration between Joe Church and some Ugandan evangelists, it fast expanded to the Presbyterian and Methodist Churches of Kenya, and then to the Mennonites and Lutherans in Tanzania in the 1940s and 1950s, taking an ecumenical shape. While the African Independent Churches created schisms within the mainstream churches and tended to be political in nature, the East African Revival Movement sought cross-denominational comity and racial harmony, albeit not without some internal tension.

During the Mau Mau period in Kenya, the revival helped to introduce a spirit of reconciliation. The leadership of the movement decried racial tension and emphasized that Africans and whites must come together to build bridges between the races. In this context, Obadiah Kariuki, an Anglican Bishop, and John Gatu, a Presbyterian cleric, both committed members of the revival, were key voices in this call, which was not well received by their European colleagues.[4]

---

3 See "Yearning behind the East African revival Movement," *Business Daily* (Dec. 13, 2018).

4 Following the account in *ibid*.

✳ ✳ ✳

The essentially egalitarian, grassroots nature of the East African Revival continues today as a fellowship in the Holy Spirit, upholding the vision and values of *koinonia*, very much along the lines described by the 1920 Lambeth Appeal. We still hear the call to fellowship in a profound way in the Diocese of Mumias where I now serve as bishop. The revival movement perdures as a regular feature of our life in the church and community. Participants focus on fellowship, prayer, conversion, confession, and sharing the Bible.

The wider Anglican Church of Kenya is built on this heritage, as well as on its cherished connection to Canterbury. With its more than four million members and global connections, the Anglican church occupies a significant space within the changing cultural, social, political, and religious landscape in Africa. The Kenyan population is disproportionately young, and Christianity shapes the ways in which many Kenyans, young and old, approach their identity, construct community, engage the world, and imagine the future.

The Lambeth Appeal's summons to fellowship connects well with our evangelical heritage and history of revival as well as with our national imagination and the African spirit. Kenya's communitarian tendencies are well known, and famously expressed in the sayings of Professor John S. Mbiti, Africa's leading scholar of religion and culture (and an Anglican): "I am because we are," and again: "because we are, therefore I am." One may find many similarly wise African proverbs, which convey this focus of our interrelatedness, both as a human and Christian family.

The 1920 Lambeth Appeal resonates with this indigenous

understanding of fellowship. The notion that we are connected through the blood of Jesus who saves us and breaks down the walls that divide is displayed publicly in the songs and testimonies of members of the East Africa Revival Movement, who meet once monthly in my diocese, bringing together Christians from six other dioceses as well as members of other denominations, including Pentecostal churches.

The decision by the primate of the Anglican Church in Kenya to allow bishops to choose for themselves to attend the 2022 Lambeth Conference because of the "historic nature of the gathering" and "for exposure" illustrates the longing in our hearts and minds to maintain connection with the wider Anglican family.[5] In the context of Communion debates around homosexuality, Africa has provided something of a strategic playing field for outside influencers, with different shades of opinion seeking to shape the African imagination. "Progressive" and "conservative" antagonists on this question have kept their eyes fixed on Africa, which commands a huge percentage of the global Anglican population, in which the average Anglican is a black woman under the age of 30.

Many bishops in my country are unhappy with positions taken by some parts of the Anglican family on same-sex relations and ministry. Yet, they also speak of the Communion's deep bonds of affection and are eager to cultivate new ties that will provide stability and encouragement for the pilgrimage.[6] We are praying that a spirit of charity

5   See the edition of *Sunday Nation* for 26 Jan. 2020.

6   See now Joseph Wandera, "Seeds of Reconciliation in Kenya" in *When Churches in Communion Disagree*, ed. Robert Heaney, Christopher Wells, and Pierre Whalon (Dallas: Living Church Books, 2022).

will pervade Lambeth Conference 2022, as it did at Lambeth 1920. Amid considerable diversity of context, we share more in common, which should form the basis for our rediscovery and experience of fellowship. This experience goes beyond us as individuals, and as putatively autonomous churches, as it is rooted in the gospel itself and in our spiritual rebirth.

Therefore, the call to fellowship is an invitation to self-realization for all of us—in Kenya and in the global family—to address our common heritage, common faith and order, and the burden each one has to be an agent of reconciliation in an increasingly broken world. This point is well expressed in Christopher Cocksworth's appeal (in chapter 11, above) to a "resonant space" and the sharing of imaginative ways of embodying communion.

I want to close on a hopeful note. The Anglican family is a great treasure, and it behooves all of us to endeavor to carry this treasure in our earthen vessels, with our eyes fixed on Jesus. Yes, we may be beaten in every way in this debate, but not crushed; perplexed, but not driven to despair; divided in the Communion but not forsaken of God (2 Cor. 4:7-10). We are on a journey with one another, in Christ. To him be the glory.

THIRTEEN

Gift and Call of Fellowship

Jane Williams

The statement of the 1920 Lambeth Conference that God wills fellowship is uncontroversial. The broad theological tradition surely unanimously affirms that fellowship is God's will for God's people.

Furthermore, there is little disagreement that God's will for fellowship in the human creation is not an arbitrary afterthought on God's part. Rather, God's will for humankind is reflective of God's being. God wills what God is. The great ecclesiological letters in the New Testament, Ephesians and Colossians, speak of this as God's purpose from before the foundation of the world, that all things will be gathered together in Christ (Eph. 1:4, 10). They also declare that this purpose has been accomplished through the death of Christ

(Col. 1:21, Eph. 2:16).[1] Matthew and Luke both start their gospels with a genealogy that highlights the work of God in Christ for the whole of humankind, which is offered salvation through Jesus Christ. John's gospel starts with the one through whom all things are made, who comes to live beside human beings so that they might become, like the Son, children of God (John 1:12). Jesus' High Priestly prayer in John 17 suggests that the unity of his followers holds up a mirror to the unity between Father and Son (John 17:21), making that unity credible to those who see the earthly mirror. The enumerating of biblical citations could go on, but there is no need to emphasize what is readily agreed by all.

In his essay, Michael Root notes the agreement between different Christian denominations on the ultimate unity of the Church, while also pointing out that disunity is caused by real theological differences. The picture he paints seems to be of a worldwide Church suffering from profound theologico-cognitive dissonance. The Church knows itself to be one, receiving its life from and witnessing to the unity of God. Yet it cannot point to or live its reality.

Ephraim Radner challenges us to find a "thicker" description of the statement that God wills fellowship. In particular, he challenges the slightly patronising undercurrent in the Lambeth Appeal of 1920, which seemed to suggest that the Anglican Communion will play a central part in God's provision of unity for the world. Although in

---

1 Ephesians is talking here of the reconciliation of Jew and Gentile through the cross, while Colossians speaks of the reconciliation between God and humanity through the cross. In both, the theme of God's reconciling, uniting purpose is undeniable.

1920 the dangers and horrors of disunity were evident, a narrative that saw God's providence at work, gifting the Anglican model of unity to a broken world, has been shown to be woefully inadequate. God not only wills—in the sense of giving—unity, but also commands it, and so requires of us our full-hearted commitment to and co-operation with the will of God in this endeavour.

Other contributors to our volume highlight the urgency of the task. Jeremiah Yang and Hannah Matis speak of the suffering of the human and non-human creation, and the sense of impending doom. We do not have time to spare. Our disunity is costing lives and, indeed, the world.

Yet the simple unavoidable fact seems to be that, although we all agree that God wills fellowship, we are not sure that God's priorities are correct. In the hundred years since the publication of the Lambeth Appeal, there are few signs of greater Church unity. The commitment to dialogue has been admirable, but the willingness to move towards greater visible unity is less obvious. All Christian denominations have more important things to do, like attempting to witness to the unity of God in a great cacophony of dissenting voices. God wills fellowship, but we do not—or only if *fellowship* means that others come to agree with *us*.

We are, then, left with a theological dilemma: God asks us of what is impossible; God commands unity that we are incapable of delivering. In all God's works toward us, God knows our weakness and gives what we cannot make for ourselves. We cannot save ourselves, overcoming the barriers between us and God, so God the Son comes to break down every barrier and inhabit our very humanity to fill it with a reconciling divine power. We cannot find in ourselves the will or ability to enter into the filial relationship that the Son offers us with the Father, through this reconciling love. The Holy Spirit comes to draw us, endlessly, through Word and Sacrament, into what is given to us. Yet it seems that we are saying that in this one thing, God will not give but merely command. God commands unity but does not give us the gifts that enable us to achieve it.

꙰ ꙰ ꙰

We are sadly resigned to this apparent state of affairs because we deceive ourselves into believing that unity between Christians is second order. We have somehow come to believe that salvation is an individual matter, so we can "be saved" without being one in Christ Jesus, although he alone is our salvation. There must, of course, be the eschatological dimension to the fullness of salvation, a dwelling in joy that cannot be anticipated now. And yet, as day by day we gather around the table of the Lord's provision and name ourselves as one body, declaring the Scriptures that draw us into God's one narrative, from creation to fulfilment, effectual through Christ, we *are* witnessing to something more than just a wistful hope for the final future. We are naming a present reality, not of our making but of God's action.

Augustine's great prayer, "Give what you command and command what you will,"[2] is a declaration about the doctrine of God. In his search for self-control, Augustine finds no hope anywhere but in the mercy of God. Furthermore, Augustine's longing for continence is not something additional, without which he can still get along

---

2 Augustine, *Confessions* X.40.

very well in his Christian discipleship. Augustine knows that this command of God is necessary for his own flourishing. Without this, Augustine will spend his life searching for beauty in the things that can only carry traces of the Beautiful, and so can never fully satisfy.

God's will that the Church should be in fellowship is the same kind of command. Without this, we cannot be Church. Without this, we are constantly searching for fellowship, for communion, for self-giving and self-receiving, in all the battered and shallow places that retain some echo of the Three who are so united that Three and One are indistinguishable. Only here may true fellowship be found.

In that case, perhaps God is not commanding the impossible but has already given us the gifts of unity in what has been provided for us as Church. The greatest gift we have already been given is God's self-gift, the Father's gift of the Son through and with the Spirit. In Word and Sacrament, the unrepeatable gift is constantly renewed. These gifts are so strangely simple that we barely notice they are shared by all Christians. They are understood differently, exercised differently, disagreed about vehemently, and yet, there they are, day in, day out: given.

❋ ❋ ❋

To be sure, the churches of the Church are still called to visible unity, which requires a wrestling with stubborn institutional divisions and seemingly settled patterns of prideful self-determination. On this count, the Anglican Communion has no particular insight into how we might more truly be the fellowship that God wills. Our bruised and battered bonds bear witness to the fact that unity is not natural to us, not something that we can find and preserve by our own effort. Perhaps our humiliation is the greatest symbol we have to offer the Christian world. There can be no complacent dependence upon a would-be Anglican Way as a bridge between churches that can only understand each other through our mediation of Catholic, Protestant, and Orthodox elements. If the Anglican Communion still lives, it is because it lives from God's self-gift, witnessed to and made present, through all our fighting, in Word and Sacrament. God has given at least part of what God wills, for the time being, as itself the way to deeper communion in him and with one another: God has given us God, in the person of the Suffering Servant.

This theological truth, and sacramental fact, sets the table for our growth in faith, hope, and love, as a call to trust God's own action in our lives and to follow where he leads, which path will pass right through all our communities taken together. St. Mellitus College, where I teach, is one small and fragile experiment in unity, one tiny adventure, among many others. It is an experiment that felt given rather than decided upon when it started, and it still feels so. Ordinands from every theological and spiritual tradition of the Church of England train together. They do not come to agree on how Word and Sacrament should be interpreted. On the contrary, they usually leave more wedded than ever to the life-giving beauty of their own strand of Anglicanism. But they also leave having witnessed the Christian discipleship of others who parse it differently. They leave with respect and, perhaps more importantly, with friendship, with fellowship, that recognises a reality greater than division, a reality of God's self-gift, that would continue to form and reform our personal and ecclesial lives, making them look more like Jesus. Only time will tell if this experiment will have any lasting effects, either on individuals or on the churches they serve, and on the one Church they and we are finally called to. But our study of the 1920 Lambeth Appeal leaves with me an overriding sense of the urgency that we answer the call to fellowship, and therefore make ourselves ready, by God's grace, to receive what he wishes to give. We need to be on high alert to this end.

Printed in Great Britain
by Amazon